UNIVERSITY OF NORTH CAROLINA
STUDIES IN THE ROMANCE LANGUAGES AND LITERATURES
Number 88

THE POETRY OF INSPIRATION
AGRIPPA D'AUBIGNE'S *LES TRAGIQUES*

THE POETRY OF INSPIRATION
AGRIPPA D'AUBIGNE'S
LES TRAGIQUES

BY

RICHARD L. REGOSIN

CHAPEL HILL
THE UNIVERSITY OF NORTH CAROLINA PRESS

DEPÓSITO LEGAL: V. 1937 - 1970

ARTES GRÁFICAS SOLER, S. A. - JÁVEA, 28 - VALENCIA (8) - 1970

To my wife Barbara,

for her confidence

ACKNOWLEDGMENTS

The present study began as a doctoral dissertation at The Johns Hopkins University. I owe a special debt to Professor Nathan Edelman who introduced me to the study of sixteenth-century French literature: to his probing, incisive questions and comments I owe much of what I have learned about d'Aubigné and the Renaissance. I am particularly grateful to Professor Lawrence Harvey for his early encouragement and continued support. I would like to thank the Editor of *Bibliothèque d'humanisme et renaissance* for permission to reprint Chapter I, which appeared in March, 1966; the Modern Language Association of America for permission to reprint Chapter II, part 1, which appeared in *PMLA* in October, 1966; and finally, Dartmouth College, for the generous assistance which made this study possible.

TABLE OF CONTENTS

	Pages
CHAPTER I. THE RESOLUTION OF DISORDER	13
I. The sword and the pen	13
II. Artistic unity	16
III. The resolution of disorder	17
CHAPTER II. DIVINE TRAGEDY	27
I. Prologue to tragedy	33
II. The poet and tragedy	39
III. The tragedy of *Les Tragiques*	41
IV. The poet as actor	51
V. The tragic ones	52
CHAPTER III. PROTESTANT APOCALYPSE	55
I. *Les Tragiques* and the Book of Revelation	55
II. Style and Apocalypse	67
CHAPTER IV. ART AND THE INSPIRED POET	79
I. The poem and the poet	80
II. Inspiration and perspective	83
III. Inspiration and metaphor	90
IV. The metaphor of sight	93
CONCLUSION	98
BIBLIOGRAPHY	104

CHAPTER I

THE RESOLUTION OF DISORDER

I

> Si jamais l'on pouvait en idée personnifier un siècle dans un individu, d'Aubigné serait, à lui seul, le type vivant, l'image abrégée du sien.[1]

Sainte-Beuve was the first to remark that the long and varied career of Agrippa d'Aubigné (1552-1630) formed an integral part of the intellectual, religious, and political fabric of France during the second half of the 16th century.[2] As a soldier who fought actively for almost thirty-five years for the Protestant cause (1568-1600), and a trusted confidant of Henry of Navarre for twenty years (1573-93), d'Aubigné played a significant role in the political and religious ferment generated by the Reformation. As a poet schooled in the humanist tradition, he shared the Renaissance esteem for the literature of antiquity and was an admirer and disciple of Ronsard and the Pléiade before turning exclusively to poetry dedicated to the Protestant cause. He was so closely identified with the spirit of his

---

[1] Sainte-Beuve, *Tableau historique et critique de la poésie française et du théâtre français au XVIe siècle* (1869), p. 140.
[2] The general biographical information in this introduction is taken from the three major biographies of d'Aubigné: A. Garnier, *Agrippa d'Aubigné et le parti protestant* (1928), 3 vols.; S. Rocheblave, *Agrippa d'Aubigné* (1910); J. Plattard, *Une figure de premier plan dans nos lettres de la Renaissance, Agrippa d'Aubigné* (1931).

age that when the times changed during the last decades of his life, d'Aubigné became a living anachronism: he still burned with a passion and zeal appropriate to a time long since past.

The composition of *Les Tragiques* grew out of the social, religious and political turmoil of the civil wars. In 1577, after having been seriously wounded in battle, d'Aubigné returned for two years to his property at Landes-Guinemer, where he composed the major part of the poem and conceived the idea for his *Histoire Universelle*.[3] Drawing from his own experience at the court and in the field, and from current histories —Crespin's *Martyrologue* (1554-70), Goulart's *Mémoires de l'estat de France sous Charles IX* (1576)— he painted a panorama of contemporary France, depicting the violence of military encounter, the virulence of religious conflict and persecution, social and economic upheaval, political and moral perversity. In these troubled times, d'Aubigné sought to comfort and encourage the Protestant faithful by disclosing God's providential design. *Les Tragiques* is a poetic vision in which the sense of history, past, present and future becomes manifest and through which the destiny of the Huguenots as the modern chosen people is made known. The victory of the true Church, unattainable on the battlefield and in the Court of France, unfolds in the world of art.

There appear to be no major 16th-century literary antecedents which influenced the composition of *Les Tragiques*.[4] For his poetic inspiration d'Aubigné returned to the literature of classical antiquity and to the Bible. The pungent sarcasm of Martial's epigrams, the violent, realistic, biting quality of Juvenal's *Satires*, written in epic hexameter, nourished the satiric style of *Les Tragiques*. The poem looks back to Tacitus and Suetonius in its focus on the royal court, and the crisp, often trenchant style recalls that of the Latin historian. From his profound knowledge of the Old Testament d'Aubigné drew the parallel between the fortunes and destiny of the Protestants and

---

[3] On the composition of *Les Tragiques* see Garnier, vol. 2, pp. 181-245.

[4] Although Ronsard's *Discours* treats the same historical period, *Les Tragiques* bears little resemblance to it. Certain of the themes and images of the *Discours* are found in *Les Tragiques*; its overall plan of composition and structure are so different, however, that the question of influence hardly arises.

those of the Hebrews.[5] He was deeply influenced by the Book of the prophet Jeremiah; the prophet's call to his people to repent, his threats of divine punishment and his lamentations, and his visions of the future all have their echoes in *Les Tragiques*. In the Revelation of St. John d'Aubigné found a correspondence between the situation of the early Christians in Rome and that of the Huguenots in France. The structure, style and content of the Book of Revelation form the essential Biblical framework of *Les Tragiques*.

During the last three decades of his life, d'Aubigné labored on his *Histoire Universelle,* attempting to attain through historical analysis and interpretation of the period 1553-1602 the end which *Les Tragiques* fulfilled in the realm of art. From direct personal experience in military, political and religious affairs of the time, from recorded documents of the religious synods and assemblies, and from contemporary histories he scrupulously documented his work, striving for historical objectivity in an effort to reveal "en la folie et la foiblesse des hommes le jugement et la force de Dieu." Here, in detail, d'Aubigné reviewed modern events and explained the destiny of his people in the light of a providential plan of history. Because the *Histoire* looked like an apology for Huguenot activities, the Catholic Church considered it propaganda. The first three volumes were condemned in Paris in 1620 and were burned in the courtyard of the Collège Royal.

D'Aubigné again put his satiric talent to work for the Protestant cause in two ironic pamphlets: *La confession catholique du sieur de Sancy* which was not published until 1660, and the *Aventures du baron de Faeneste* which appeared in 1616 and 1617.[6] The *Confession* parodies the apologies which were published by Huguenots who converted to Catholicism following the abjuration of Henry IV. The success of its ironic style depends on restraint (as opposed to the energy and violence of *Les Tragiques*), but d'Aubigné could not deal with this subject without losing his self-control, and often the sarcasm dissolves into bitter invective. In the *Faeneste,* the poet ridicules the provincial manners and speech of the boisterous

---

[5] This was a widely held notion which d'Aubigné was able to document through his intimate knowledge of the Bible.
[6] See Garnier, pp. 245-68; Rocheblave, pp. 146-78; Plattard, pp. 75-92.

Gascon; the customs and costumes of the courtiers are equally the butt of his sharp humor.

Except for the years spent languishing for Diane Salviati (1570-73), and those at the court of the Valois (1573-76) —years which he later scorned as wasted in idleness— the efforts and accomplishments which define d'Aubigné's life drew their inspiration from a single source: devotion to the Protestant cause. From the age of eight, when his father made him swear an oath before the mutilated bodies of the Huguenot martyrs of the Amboise conspiracy to dedicate himself to his religion, this purpose infused d'Aubigné's activity. As a soldier he fought for the success of the true Christian faith; as a poet he attempted to realize this triumph through art. The unity of his literary achievement lies in the common purpose it sought to fulfill. Whether visionary poetry, like that of *Les Tragiques,* satiric prose like the *Confession* and *Faeneste,* or religious and political history like the *Histoire Universelle,* each of d'Aubigné's serious works continues the struggle he began with the sword.

II

This link between d'Aubigné's life and his literary effort lends support to the traditional emphasis which has been placed on the biographical and historical aspects of *Les Tragiques*. Critics such as Plattard and Garnier —who regarded art as the re-presentation of reality— applied their knowledge of the author and his times to elucidate countless references in the poem and, conversely, interpreted the poem to give us a better sense of the tenor of the time. From another point of view though, the mimetic approach impoverished our understanding of *Les Tragiques*: because it never considered the work as a poetic entity, it failed to appreciate its artistic unity. A. Tilley's terse remark that the poem is "badly planned as a whole without any semblance of unity" is typical of the judgments of its literary merit.[7] Not until Herman Gmelin's study in 1937, and more significantly Henry Sauerwein's 1953 thesis,

---

[7] A. Tilley, *The Literature of the French Renaissance* (1904), vol. 2, p. 259.

was the unity of *Les Tragiques* clearly established and the longstanding charge of obscurity refuted.[8]

Dr. Sauerwein's study of the poetic structure of *Les Tragiques* revealed that the literal narrative, which builds up structure in terms of a plan of composition, represented a coherent, integrated progression from the unnatural situation in "Misères" to the final restoration of order in "Jugement." At the same time it uncovered a supraliteral development which reflects a structure in the actual poetic language. Sauerwein found that pivotal words and images were endowed with connotations and associations which allowed the poet, by the use of one image or leit-motif, to evoke a mass of suggested meanings. These clusters fall into two patterns ranged against each other in a conflict which reproduces the literal struggle in the poem between Catholics and Protestants. Within the realm of art the poet transcends the unresolved strife of historical reality to effect the triumph of the true Christian Church.

Dr. Sauerwein's thesis is primarily concerned with the examination of these word clusters. Despite its ungainly and bewildering statistical, accumulative and repetitious manner of presentation, it offers a valuable starting point for discussions of d'Aubigné's poetic strategy. It points up the theme of *Les Tragiques* as the resolution of disorder, which must be broadened, and re-examined here by way of introduction.

III

The first book of *Les Tragiques*, "Misères," defines the death and destruction wrought by the civil wars consuming France as an evil that is unnatural. The ideals of ordered nature, of inherent bonds of familial love, of peace and prosperity which the poet longingly evokes (279-88; 563-80) are shattered as Frenchman struggles against brother Frenchman and as both sons turn on their mother, France.[9] Parents desert their offspring (356), fathers strangle

---

[8] H. Gmelin, "D'Aubigné als Dichter französischen Schicksals," *Neuphilologische Monatsschrift*, VIII (1937), 33-56; H. Sauerwein, *Agrippa d'Aubigné's Les Tragiques* (1953).

[9] Agrippa d'Aubigné, *Les Tragiques*, eds. A. Garnier et J. Plattard (1932). References to the poem will be made by book in roman numerals, by line

their sons (212), and children rise up against their parents (236). This perversion is forcefully expressed by the use of animal images which dehumanize man: France has become a horrible beast (157), the kings, wolves feeding on their flock, and the peasants seeking safety in the forests animals living in caves, subsisting on roots and berries (312-14). Rape and murder have replaced civil law (217), and injustice reigns as justice (235): the judge is dragged into court where the criminal sits in judgment. Even the Salic law, the law of laws (736), is broken with Catherine de Medici on the throne.

The presentation of this *monde à l'envers* (235) draws its expressive force in part from the significance given to order and family in the Calvinist doctrine which formed d'Aubigné's religious background. At the foundation of the Huguenot's faith is the reality of divine providence, of God, the Good, causing and disposing all things. The faithful, confident that he is in God's hands and assured of the essential order and design of human existence, gives himself to his Lord. Calvin appears to acknowledge an order inherent in human nature and the inclination of man's reason toward an ordered social life:

> L'intention de Dieu est qu'on observe l'ordre de nature. [10]

> Entant que l'homme est de nature compagnable, il est aussi enclin d'une affection naturelle à entretenir et conserver société. Pourtant nous voyons qu'il y a quelques cogitations généralles d'une honnesteté et ordre civil imprimées en l'entendement de tous hommes. [11]

These qualities, which contrast with Calvin's emphasis on man's total moral depravity, derive nonetheless from the gift of general grace which God grants to all mankind.

---

in arabic numerals. D'Aubigné entitled the books, however, as follows: I, Misères; II, Princes; III, Chambre Dorée; IV, Feux; V, Fers; VI, Vengeances; VII, Jugement.

[10] J. Calvin, "Sermon CXXVII sur le Deutéronome, Chap. XXII," *Joannis Calvini Opera quae supersunt omnia*. ed. G. Baum, E. Cunitz, E. Reuss (1892), vol. 28, p. 31.

[11] J. Calvin, *Institution de la religion chrestienne*, ed. Abel Lefranc (1911), Chap. II, p. 54. This text of the *Institution* is the 1541 French translation of the second edition of the Latin text published in Strasbourg in 1539.

Behind the notion of providence is the belief that God's principal attribute is his paternity, the loving-kindness He feels for His children. Human family unity derives its essence from this bond: "Nous ne saurons que c'est du devoir de père envers les enfans, ne de la reverance des enfans envers leurs pères et superieurs, sinon que Dieu est le degré souverain." [12] He who perverts the family relationship revolts against God and becomes a monster, outside of the natural.

The introduction of the religious *monde à l'envers* (1207) parallels the presentation of disorder in national terms. The Protestant Church is portrayed in an unnatural position: banished from the world (695) and held captive under the altars of the idols (13-14). The Pope, who is pictured first as an enemy of France (1209-14), emerges as the mortal adversary of the Church, the antichrist who claims for himself the role of God on earth (1239-44).

The image clusters which Dr. Sauerwein uncovers in "Misères" draw the lines of this conflict between Protestants and Catholics. The evocation of Rome, the use of images of fire and the vocabulary of beasts relate Catherine de Medici and her nobles, the Pope and Italy to the Emperor Nero, the persecutor of the early Christians. On the other side, the image clusters group France and the Huguenots as lambs, thus calling up Christ, the protagonist of the Antichrist and of Satan.

In the last lines of "Misères" we find an image which vividly communicates the disorder of the *monde à l'envers*. The Huguenot is ready to praise God with song and with the music of the lute, but his fingers are tied and his voice is hoarse:

> Tel est en cest estat le tableau de l'Eglise...
>   Tu aimes de ses mains la parfaicte harmonie:
> Nostre luth chantera le principe de vie;
> Nos doigts ne sont plus doigts que pour trouver tes sons,
> Nos voix ne sont plus voix qu'à tes sainctes chansons.
>   Mets à couvert ces voix que les pluyes enrouënt:
> Deschaine donc ces doigts, que sur ton luth ils jouënt.
> (1341-50)

A perverse world precludes the existence of music, which is a

---

[12] J. Calvin, "Sermon CLXI sur le Deutéronome, Chap. XXVIII," *Opera,* vol. 28, p. 454.

symbol of harmony and order. Before music can be heard again, the disorder must be resolved.[13]

Book two, "Princes," attacks and exposes the cruelty and perversion of the Valois court. With the light of truth as his guide, the poet unmasks the false counselors and flatterers who have beguiled the kings and corrupted virtue and justice. He then turns his scorn upon the monarchs, whose attempts to disguise the horror and carnage they have created have taken the form of masquerades and comedies, foolish and licentious games. Henri III symbolizes the disorder of the *monde à l'envers*. His femininity and homosexuality, as perversions of nature, stamp him as a monster, outside the bounds of the natural.

The metaphorical structure of "Princes" sustains and broadens that of the first book by relating the iniquitous counselors and kings to the group of negative images: Catholic, Pope, Catherine, Nero, beast. The false advisors and cruel monarchs are pictured as bestial, inhuman, unnatural monsters identified by their sexual perversion. The motif light-darkness, introduced in "Princes," expands the alignment of images significantly: truth and virtue are presented as light, sun and flame and are opposed to the darkness of the court (Avernus), the activities of the princes (*noires ordures*) and the false luster of disguise and make-up which obscures and distorts reality. Finally, the allegorical confrontation of Fortune and Virtue which comprises the second section of the book associates cowardice, shame and luxury with the Catholic party, modesty, sobriety and simplicity with Henri IV, Coligny and the virtuous Protestants.

"Chambre Dorée" forms a poetic bloc with "Princes": it sustains the allegorical element in the opposition between Justice and Injustice; it begins the resolution of the disorder of Book II; it develops the image clusters of "Princes." Focusing on the false judges, the poet represents them as beasts and unnatural monsters and their justice as false luster. The allegorical presentation of the vices which hold sway in the Palais de Justice further enriches the image clusters of Books I and II by recalling the darkness of Avernus, the make-up and hypocrisy of the flatterers and the bestiality of the princes. The poet's attack on the Spanish court

---

[13] See L. Spitzer, *Classical and Christian Ideas of World Harmony* (1963), p. 134 for d'Aubigné and the musical unity of the world.

links it through metaphor with Italy, Nero, the Pope and Satan and sets it against Christ and the meek of the earth embodied in Queen Elizabeth of England. At the close of "Chambre Dorée" the entire dramatic alignment is clearly apparent: wolf/Nero/ Pope/Antichrist/ Catholicism (Italy, Spain) /Catherine /injustice/ unnatural against Lamb/Christ/Protestantism (England, the France of the Huguenots) /Elizabeth/Justice/nature.

The last half of "Chambre Dorée" (695-1060) discloses the truth of the restoration of order by presenting a vision of the eventual triumph of the just, symbolized by Themis, the goddess of law and order, and the damnation of the wicked, represented by Nemesis, law and order avenging itself on the wicked. This presentation parallels the earlier picture of Injustice and her court (249-512) and is analogous to the confrontation of Fortune and Virtue: order, nature and truth are opposed to perversity, evil and disorder and in both cases true values reveal the sham of the false. The order which Themis symbolizes now exists only in Heaven, but its realization on earth is inevitable and immanent: "Rien n'arreste les pas de la blanche Themis" (888). The positive figure of Elizabeth at the close of "Chambre Dorée" reinforces the sense of the coming resolution of disorder expressed in the psalmist's prayer for vengeance at the end of the book:

> Le bras de l'Eternel, aussi doux que robuste,
> Fait du mal au meschant et fait du bien au juste,
> Et en terre ici bas exerce jugement
> En attendant le jour de peur et tremblement.
>
> (1051-54)

"Feux" presents a poetic history of Protestant martyrdom in terms of a conflict between the haughty and the meek (*grands* and *petits*) in which the humble children of God emerge victorious. The fire by which the iniquitous punish the Protestant "heretics" provides the means to triumph over physical death (93-94): it cleanses the soul making it worthy of salvation (14) and carries it to eternal life in Heaven ("...il vole/Porter dedans le ciel et l'ame et la parole" 205-206). Through martyrdom, physical death in a human context becomes rebirth within a spiritual framework: "Ainsi la noire mort donna la claire vie" (541).

This triumph of the just, which has been preordained from the beginning of time (10), rests on the doctrine of predestination to which Calvin turned to comfort his persecuted followers. Since the faithful have been chosen for salvation *ab aeterno ante mundi constitutionem,* they are in God's hands. The events of their lives are meaningful in terms of that assured end, and they can thus confidently withstand Catholic hostility and persecution:

> Si les fideles ne sont pas fermement attachés à cette arche sainte, à savoir que Dieu les a eleus de toute eternité à cause de Christ, jamais ils ne resisteront au milieu des flots et des attaques de Satan et du monde. [14]

The suffering which the elect endure is part of the providential order: it allows them to overcome self-love and self-exaltation and to give themselves to God. Through it, God tests and purifies His children to lead them to eternal life in Heaven:

> Si nous recevons opprobre et ignominie, nous sommes d'autant plus exaltés au royaume de Dieu. Si nous mourons, l'ouverture nous est faite en la vie bienheureuse. [15]

The poet employs the metaphor of the seasons to characterize the evolution of the true Church. After the spring of its birth —the era of the Hebrews— and the summer of full bloom —Christ and the early Christians— the Protestant epoch represents the autumn. Traditionally, autumn is the last flowering, the period of maturity passing into the decline which precedes winter's old age and death. The images of Themis and Nemesis in the third book, the deaths of the martyrs which presage the punishment of the wicked, the apocalyptic vision of Elect souls under the altars awaiting vengeance imply that an end is at hand. The winter of the Church, however, will not be the traditional season of destruction. It will be the end of terrestrial perversity and disorder in final judgment, and the emergence of the harmony of the celestial universe where Heaven and Hell will be the eternal recompense.

---

[14] Cited in E. Doumergue, *Jean Calvin* (1910), vol. 4, p. 412.
[15] J. Calvin, *Institution, op. cit.,* Chap. XVII, p. 806.

The civil wars raging in France which form the literal subject matter of "Fers" are a reflection of the more essential conflict between God and Satan. In the first four books of *Les Tragiques,* evil has been worked through diabolical agents — Catherine, the Pope, the wicked princes and false judges. The opening scene of "Fers" where God allows Satan to declare all-out war, and the concentration of unnatural motifs in this description of supreme evil, show Satan to be the single source of iniquity.

The *tableaux* of terrestrial events painted in Heaven, which the poet is privileged to view and describe, indicate the victory of the humble, the Lamb and the spiritual life over the forces of Satan. The St. Bartholomew's Day massacre occupies the center of attention because of the apparently meaningless slaughter of innocent thousands. Through Biblical analogy (521-28) the poet points out that life for the Protestants represents a journey similar to the Hebrews' exodus from Egypt, their wandering through the desert and their arrival in the land of Canaan. God watches over His children, protecting and guiding them as they endure the suffering and hardship which characterize the road to eternal salvation. This interpretation of the persecution of the faithful is in harmony with the traditional Calvinist doctrine of *renoncement* and *la vie chrestienne*:

> Tous ceux que le Seigneur a adoptez et receus en la compaignie de ses enfans se doyvent preparer à une vie dure, laborieuse, pleine de travail et de infiniz genres de maux. C'est le bon plaisir du Père celeste, de exercer ainsi ses serviteurs à fin de les experimenter. Il a commencé cest ordre en Christ, son Filz premier nay, et le poursuit envers tous les autres. [16]

At the end of "Fers," the poet describes a vision in which an angel of God discloses Heaven's secrets to reveal the forthcoming destruction of the iniquitous: "Voy de Jerusalem la nation remise,/ l'Antechrist abattu, en triomphe l'Eglise" (1413-14). This divine prophecy guarantees the final restoration of order toward which the poem has been progressing, and goes as far as to fix the year in

---

[16] *Ibid.,* p. 800.

which it will take place: "...car le Grand Juge en son throsne est assis/Si tost que l'aere joinct à nos mille trois six" (1415-16).

"Vengeances" and "Jugement" form a poetic bloc which is the climax of *Les Tragiques*. By the end of "Fers," the contemporary *monde à l'envers* has been made intelligible and the outcome of every conflict on the supra-literal level has been decided: Lamb over wolf, meek over haughty, truth, justice and light over hypocrisy, injustice and obscurity. Although the clusters appear through the last two books, they are no longer contending. They are elements in the final cosmic triumph of good over evil, God over Satan, which is accomplished through God's role as *juste vengeur*, and through the final judgment. "Vengeances" describes divine retribution during the "Eglise Primitive," the "Première Eglise" and modern times to warn the wicked and comfort the righteous that the end of time is at hand. The recurrent prayer of the captive souls for the restoration of order through the punishment of the iniquitous is finally to be answered:

> Leve ton bras de fer, haste tes pieds de laine,
> Venge ta patience en l'aigreur de la peine.
>
> (I, 1377-78)

> Pren ta verge de fer, tracasse de tes fleaux
> La machoire fumante à ces fiers lionceaux.
>
> (III, 1033-34)

> O Dieu, puissant vengeur, tes mains seront ostees
> De ton sein, car ceci du haut ciel tu verras
> Et de cent mille morts à poinct te vengeras.
>
> (V, 360-62)

The enactment of divine vengeance symbolizes the return of order by recalling the form and severity of the original crimes: "...tous pechez ont les vengeances telles/Que merite le faict" (790-91). The castigation of Nebuchadnezzar exemplifies the punishment of all persecuting kings. He is called a *Roi non Roi* and an *homme-beste* and is physically reduced to the bestial level on which he lived. The worldly success of the Roman emperors is rendered illusory by the ignominious deaths they endure. The *persecuteurs de l'Eglise Première* march enchained under the banner of the triumphant Lamb.

The modern iniquitous, unlike their predecessors, have directed their efforts against the soul rather than the body of the Church. Disguised as priests, counselors and magistrates, they have professed the Gospel while martyrizing the true Christians. To punish this most vicious of all persecutions God destroys the wicked by hail, fire and brimstone in an act of universal, temporal vengeance:

> Ici le haut tonnant sa voix grosse hors met,
> Et gresle et souffre et feu sur la terre transmet,
> Fait la charge sonner par l'airain du tonnerre;
> Il a la mort, l'enfer, soudoyez pour sa guerre.
>
> (1123-26)

The way is now ready for God to make his descent to earth for the Last Judgment.

The first part of "Jugement" (1-340) anticipates the dispensing of ultimate justice. The poet recalls the story of Gideon (39) representing God differentiating between the Elect and the abandoned. This spiritual ordering is reflected in the spatial arrangement of the celestial universe which places the good on the right of God, the wicked on His left, and in the vision which reverses the persecution of the Protestants to make them the instrument of divine retribution (63-80). The long passage confirming the resurrection of the body (341-660) contributes to the symbolic resolution of disorder. This rebirth, and the fire and brimstone of the Christian Hell, guarantee that the wicked will be physically punished by the ordered analogue of their own auto-da-fé (327-28). It allows the reunion of body and soul, created for each other and separated at death (655-58). Resurrection reflects as well the restoration to proper functioning of nature and its laws. As the flowers which appear to have died during the winter bloom again in the spring, so man's body comes to life after apparent destruction (523-26.)

After the immortality of the soul and the resurrection of the flesh are posited as unquestionable truths, the actual judgment unfolds as a vision taking place before the poet's very eyes. First, the destruction of the old world *à l'envers* makes way for the creation of the kingdom of Heaven: "L'autre ciel, l'autre terre ont cependant fuï,/Tout ce qui fut mortel se perd esvanouï" (709-10). With the lambs on the right dressed in white, and the wolves on the left, God passes eternal judgment, damning and rewarding in terms which invert the world of disorder. God has become a tyrant for the wicked, reducing them from fierce and proud lions and wolves to *lions de torches aculés* and *loups emmuzelés* (765-66). The good, made kings —"Leur Roy donc les appelle et les fait rois ainsi" (870)— experience perfect love (1105), perfect memory (1144) and perfect knowledge of things (1141). Each soul acquires a perfect knowledge of God according to its own capacity. The music of the lutes, silent since "Misères," can be heard once again in the celestial *monde à l'endroit*:

> Faut-il des sons? le Grec qui jadis s'est vanté
> D'avoir ouï les cieux, sur l'Olympe monté,
> Seroit ravi plus haut quand cieux, orbes et poles
> Servent aux voix des Saincts de luths et de violes.
>
> (1185-88)

The development of the poem, from the terrestrial disorder of "Misères" to the celestial order of "Jugement," from the apparent victory of the iniquitous to the ultimate triumph of the just culminates as the poet is assumed, living, into immortality at the end of history. The vision of final judgment becomes reality in his ascent to Heaven:

> Mes sens n'ont plus de sens, l'esprit de moy s'envole,
> Le coeur ravi se taist, ma bouche est sans parole:
> Tout meurt, l'ame s'enfuit, et reprenant son lieu
> Exstatique se pasme au giron de son Dieu.
>
> (1215-18)

CHAPTER II

DIVINE TRAGEDY

D'Aubigné scholars have perpetuated the notion that the many references to "tragédie" and "tragiques" in *Les Tragiques* are unrelated to any generic concept of tragedy. Preoccupied with the biographical and historical aspects of the poem, nineteenth-century literary historians either neglected —like Lanson and Tilley— to face the questions raised by the presence of these references in an epic context, or offered —like Faguet— a vague suggestion that the work contains certain "vers de tragédie." More recent critics have been concerned with the artistic unity of the epic poem, and appear, for the sake of that unity, to have ruled out the possibility of a fusion of the epic and tragic genres. The consensus, as expressed by Henry Sauerwein, is that within the context of the poem, "tragédie" and "tragique" are descriptive terms which refer to situations of misery, suffering, and bloody hardship in the civil and religious conflict.[1] Henri Weber denies any resemblance between the progression of the action of *Les Tragiques* and what he calls the "récit dramatique" of tragedy.[2] For the modern critic then, as well as for his nineteenth-century predecessors, *Les Tragiques* bears little or no relationship to dramatic tragedy.

Such interpretations, however, do not satisfactorily explain the prominence of so many terms related to tragedy as a dramatic genre. D'Aubigné's opening invocation is not to the epic muse but to Melpomene, the muse of tragedy (I, 79). He indicates that the

---

[1] H. Sauerwein, *Agrippa d'Aubigné's Les Tragiques* (1953), pp. 107-108.
[2] H. Weber, *La création poétique au XVIe siècle en France* (1956), p. 727.

cothurnus —the high boot worn by the actors in Greek tragedy—
is appropriate to his subject (I, 78). We learn that on the "triste
eschaffaut" —the stage where the action takes place— the role of
death will be played by Death herself (I, 76).[3] The poet addresses
his contemporaries in these terms: "Voyez la tragedie, abbaissez
vos courages,/ Vous n'estes spectateurs, vous estes personnages" (I,
169-70). The very title of the work, *Les Tragiques,* compellingly
invites interpretation. An analysis of "tragédie" and "tragique"
within the thematic and structural framework of the poem, and
against the background of 16th-century notions of tragedy, suggests
the need for revising the traditional view.

The literary tenor of the closing decades of the 16th century did
not dictate a clearly defined concept of tragedy, nor did it uni-
formly require the separation of the tragic and epic genres. D'Aubigné was thus free to assume his personal poetic stance, drawing
upon the differing views offered him by the heirs of the medieval tradition, the partisans of Greek and Latin literature, the students of
Aristotle and the Protestant tragedians. Guided by the exigencies
of his subject and his own inclination, he was eclectic in his choice.
Although he turned for the most part from the literary notions of
Ronsard and the Pléiade (whose import is evident in his "Printemps") to the medieval tradition they disdained, his humanist's
appreciation of the literature of antiquity continued unabated and
the influence of Greek tragedy and of Aristotle as seen through the
eyes of Jean de la Taille is manifest in *Les Tragiques.*[4]

D'Aubigné's vision of the contemporary world represented a
spectacle which he evidently felt was most appropriate to presentation as tragedy. Yet the universal drama which he saw taking place
between God and Satan, the Protestant and Catholic Churches, was
inconsistent with the Pléiade's concept of tragedy, which insisted on
verisimilitude and the consequent rejection of allegory. Peletier's
implication that tragedy is a dramatic form likewise appears to

---

[3] In the 16th century "eschaffaut" meant stage as well as death scaffold.
See E. Huguet, *Dictionnaire de la langue française du XVIe siècle* (1925),
Vol. 3, pp. 593-94.

[4] For the influence of Ronsard and the Pléiade on d'Aubigné see M.
Raymond, *L'influence de Ronsard sur la poésie française* (1927), Vol. 2,
pp. 314-20 and *Agrippa d'Aubigné: Le Printemps,* ed. H. Weber (1960),
pp. 5-37.

have precluded any fusion of tragedy with the epic, although the latter genre was compatible with the temporal and spatial dimension of the action of *Les Tragiques* and with the presence of the marvelous. Scaliger's views created the same impasse, for while allowing gods to people the epic (*Poetices Libri Septem*, III, 96), they limited tragedy to drama — a play in which characters act and gesture on a stage (I, 3).

The medieval tradition, based on the Latin grammarians Diomedes and Donatus and perpetuated in the Renaissance by such writers as Guillaume Bouchetel, Lazare de Baïf and Thomas Sebillet, did not, however, include a dramatic requirement in its definition of tragedy.[5] Although Diomedes had differentiated between dramatic and narrative poetry, and although he had spoken of "tragica" and "comica" as dramatic genres of the Greeks, he had not included this dramatic element in his definition of the genres. In medieval dictionaries neither tragedy nor comedy is defined as a "dramaticum genus," a fact that elucidates the strange confusion in the Middle Ages between epic poems and comedies.[6] When Dante explains his choice of the title *Commedia*, the reasons he gives comprise the traditional definition of comedy.[6a] Although the medieval heritage was quickly losing ground in the latter half of the 16th century to the influence of classical antiquity, it still represented an authoritative aspect of the current literary framework. D'Aubigné appears to have acknowledged this absence of generic distinction by basing *Les Tragiques* on the overlap between tragic and epic structure and content, thus achieving a form suited to the nature of his subject.[7]

The medieval heritage also justifies calling *Les Tragiques* a tragedy. Although the traditional fatal dénouement is missing, the

---

[5] See G. Lanson, "L'idée de la tragédie en France avant Jodelle," *RHL*, 11 (1904), 541-585, for the influence of the medieval tradition in the Renaissance, including its effect on those who, like Peletier and Scaliger, rejected it outright.

[6] E. Kern, *The Influence of Heinsius and Vossius upon French Dramatic Theory* (1949), p. 21.

[6a] Letter to Can Grande. Quoted from Kern, *ibid.*, p. 22.

[7] It is significant perhaps that among the books in d'Aubigné's library was Dante's *Divina Commedia* which too owes its form to this overlap of the genres. See A. Garnier, *Agrippa d'Aubigné et le parti protestant* (1928), Vol. 3, p. 203.

inclusion of any of the other distinguishing characteristics —historical subject of bloody horror, illustrious characters, nobility of style— sufficed to make the work a tragedy.[8] The temporal and spatial scope of *Les Tragiques,* its allegorical figures, the presence of God and the angels, and its didactic nature recall the structure and content of the medieval morality which Sebillet and others considered the French counterpart of ancient tragedy:

> La Moralité Françoise represente en quelque chose la Tragedie Greque et Latine, singulièrement en ce qu'elle traitte fais graves et Principaus. Et si le François s'estoit rangé à ce que la fin de la Moralité fut toujours triste et douloureuse, La Moralité seroit Tragedie...[9]

D'Aubigné's subject required a felicitous ending to the action, and here, for precedent, the poet might have turned to the current vogue of the tragi-comedy, to Scaliger's or la Taille's reading of Aristotle or to Protestant tragedies like those of Bèze or Rivaudeau.[10]

Certain parallels between Jean de la Taille's *Art de la tragedie* (1572) and *Les Tragiques* (and others which will be established at a later point in this work) imply that la Taille's interpretation of Aristotle, more than any other single work, influenced the content, structure and purpose of the poem. The historical proximity of the two works —the *Art de la tragedie* was published five years before the inception of *Les Tragiques*— and the common religious, social, political and literary background which the two Protestant soldier-poets shared make this influence even more likely. Unlike most of his contemporaries, la Taille proposed the affective reaction of the spectator as the purpose of tragedy: "la vraye et seule intention d'une tragedie est d'esmouvoir et de poindre merveilleusement les affections d'un chascun."[11] D'Aubigné echoes these words in his

---

[8] Lanson, *op. cit.,* p. 554.

[9] T. Sebillet, *Art poétique françoys,* ed. F. Gaiffe (1910), p. 161.

[10] Henry Lancaster points out in *The French Tragi-Comedy* (1907) that the happy dénouement was the chief characteristic of the popular 16th-century tragi-comedy. "During the sixteenth century, the name could be applied to any play of medieval origin which possessed a happy dénouement and a form that was at least partially classic" (p. xxiv). As the idea that the felicitous outcome was consistent with tragedy became established in France, the tragi-comedy began to decline, and practically ceased to exist after 1657.

[11] Jean de la Taille, *Art de la tragédie,* ed. F. West (1939), p. 24.

Préface where he avows his intention to move his audience: "Nous sommes ennuyés de livres qui enseignent, donnez-nous en pour esmouvoir." In practice the poem does not abandon the didactic function of art as it strives to reveal the divine meaning of history. But the poet instructs in order to bring consolation and joy to the faithful, to awaken sorrow and pity in the hearts of the indifferent, to arouse terror in the breasts of the iniquitous.

La Taille's conception of the structure of tragedy is defined in terms of its ability to stir the emotions:

> Or c'est le principal point d'une Tragedie de la sçavoir bien disposer, bien bastir, et la deduire de sorte qu'elle change, transforme, manie et tourne l'esprit des escoutans de ça de là, et faire qu'ils voyent maintenant une joye tournée tout soudain en tristesse, et maintenant au rebours, à l'exemple des choses humaines. [12]

Clearly the verbs *disposer*, *bastir* and *deduire*, together with the change of fortune of *une joye tournée tout soudain en tristesse... et au rebours* stress, as in Aristotle, the primacy of action. La Taille's other statements, although they too are vague and general indications of plot construction, bear the same emphasis: "Qu'elle (la tragédie) soit bien entre-lassée, meslée, entre-coupée, reprise et surtout à la fin portée à quelque resolution et but." [13] Unlike contemporary theory and practice of dramatic tragedy which accentuated character and the exposition of suffering and passion, la Taille appears to stress a tightly knit, unified plot composed of intimately related action and events and structured around numerous changes in fortune which move the spectator. The tragic effect is achieved by the disposition of action rather than the felicitous or fatal ending of the drama. As in Aristotle, change in fortune is a more significant affective element than the simple destruction of the hero.

The dramatic action of *Les Tragiques* fulfills the requirements stated by la Taille. In the course of the action, France and the Protestant Church experience a change of fortune from misery to happiness while the Catholics undergo the opposite peripeteia. As the poet moves between the terrestrial and celestial perspectives,

---

[12] *Ibid.*, pp. 26-27.
[13] *Ibid.*, p. 27.

individuals or groups of individuals are brought low or raised to the heavenly heights. The spectator is faced with constant movement and change to which he responds with a variety of emotional reactions. In fact, all the possible subjects which la Taille suggests as proper for tragedy play a major role in the poem: the fall of great heroes, the vicissitudes of fortune, wars, plagues, and the cruelty of tyrants. Finally, the structure of *Les Tragiques* is defined by action: the action which is the revolt of Satan and the iniquitous against Heaven; the action of persecution; that of the resistance of God and the Huguenots; and most important, the action initiated by the poet himself as he becomes a participant. Although it is possible that d'Aubigné had direct access to one of the texts of Aristotle's *Poetics* published in France during the middle decades of the 16th century, such evidence makes it more likely that he knew the Greek master through la Taille's *Art de la tragedie*.[14]

But d'Aubigné did not slavishly imitate la Taille. Rather he appears to have dismissed those elements which did not conform to the nature of his subject: the implication that tragedy is dramatic, the role of the chorus, the requirement of verisimilitude. At the same time, his understanding of the nature of Greek tragedy went beyond what he might have learned from la Taille. D'Aubigné's appreciation of the role of pride and the ambiguous position of the tragic hero who is at once guilty and innocent, responsible agent and victim, recalls la Taille's notion that the hero be neither a very good nor a very bad man, and suggests that he had perhaps studied the Greek texts of Sophocles and Euripides. His presentation of supernatural characters was consistent with ancient tragedy which, as drama, did bring in gods and the marvelous.

D'Aubigné's success in integrating Biblical subject matter into classical form resulted in part from an awareness of the earlier attempts of certain Protestant tragedians to bring together the material of the Bible and the form of tragedy. From Théodore de Bèze's *Abraham sacrifiant* (1550) d'Aubigné would have learned the necessity of subordinating considerations of form to the requirements of the didactic and propagandist purpose of his work. Bèze's desire to portray the faith of God's Elect and to assure His children of

---

[14] For the editions of the *Poetics* in France during the 16th century see Spingarn, *Literary Criticism in the Renaissance* (1899), pp. 183-85.

the Lord's grace determined the choice of characters, the nature of the action, and the resulting felicitous dénouement. Perhaps a more striking lesson would have been André de Rivaudeau's *Aman* (1565). His attempt to preserve the integrity of both classical form and Biblical content led Rivaudeau to a clouding of both the preceptive purpose demanded by the religious aspect and the aesthetic function of the tragic elements. From a classical point of view Aman approximates the tragic hero who in his pride challenges God and undergoes a reversal of fortune in which he loses his life. From the didactic perspective the long suffering, faithful Hebrews are the heroes and Aman remains the totally bad villain. D'Aubigné avoided the pitfalls of *Aman* by choosing a religious subject which according to la Taille's theory and practice was proper for presentation as tragedy. While adhering to the view of tragedy which allows a fortunate ending, he was able to approximate the nature and action of the Greek tragic hero in his own attempt to examine the relationship of man to God, fusing the vital non-dramatic aspects of ancient tragedy with his religious material and the didactic and affective purpose of his poem.

I

The opening verses of "Misères," which describe the subject matter of the poem, introduce aspects of tragedy even before the expression "tragédie" appears:

> Ici le sang n'est feint, le meurtre n'y defaut,
> La mort jouë elle-mesme en ce triste eschaffaut,
> Le Juge criminel tourne et emplit son urne.
> D'ici la botte en jambe, et non pas le cothurne,
> J'appelle Melpomene en sa vive fureur...
> (I, 75-79)

Within the context of an epic, d'Aubigné intends a drama—action on a stage with roles and characters—to take place. The invocation to Melpomene and the mention of the cothurnus, to which I have alluded, indicate that the dramatic action will be a tragedy. This is reinforced by the poetic richness of "eschaffaut," which in this framework juxtaposes the meanings of stage where the scene takes place and death scaffold: the play will present subject matter characterized by blood and murder, and death herself will be one of the principal characters. The events of *Les Tragiques,* unlike the love poetry the poet had been writing to this time, do not represent a world of fiction drawn from the imagination of the artist: the blood is real blood, the murdered really die, and death plays herself. The exterior world inhabits the realm of art. The muse, who is a poetic, metaphorical figure, here arises wildly out of the real wars raging about her, "eschevelée, affreuse, et bramant" (I, 82). The poet sees her as awakening out of "tombeaux" which he grimly describes as "rafraischis"—or dug up again to receive the swarming new victims, and, one readily gathers at the same time, stirred up again by the poet in order to conjure up the gruesome spectacle.

"Misères" serves as a narrative exposé of the tragedy as it has progressed to the present. It sets the stage on which the drama is being played, presents the principal characters, and defines the nature of the tragic action. It covers those acts of the play which represent the complication of the tragic plot and carries the action to the point where the actual dramatic tragedy contained in *Les Tragiques* begins. The "tragedy" in the poem is then the dénouement of the events whose progression has been recorded in the historical narrative of this first book. The epic form allows the poet to integrate this background matter into the body of the work itself.

The poet evokes the muse of tragedy and her words introduce France as the first significant tragic character:

> O France desolee! ô terre sanguinaire,
> Non pas terre, mais cendre! ô mere, si c'est mere
> Que trahir ses enfans aux douceurs de son sein
> Et quand on les meurtrit les serrer de sa main!
>
> (I, 89-92)

This portrait accuses France, the mother, of being responsible for the deaths of her two sons, the Catholic and Protestant parties. But the "terre sanguinaire" is also a "France desolee," and versions of the same metaphor reproach the children for the murder of their mother. After the muse has expressed the one possibility: "ô mere! si c'est mere / Que trahir ses enfans..." the poet probes further, and chooses to stress also the other possibility or truth: "Je veux peindre la France une mere affligee" (I, 97). As the poet employs various images to describe the condition of France, he maintains this ambiguity between her role as victim and that of responsible party. When she is depicted as the giant who turns against itself, she is guilty of her own demise, for she becomes a victim of her greatness (I, 133-62). Yet, as the helpless mother murdered by marauding soldiers, she is the innocent victim: "ce corps seché, retraict / De la France qui meurt" (I, 423-24). France is the sufferer again when as a ship she sinks because of the two warring parties on board (I, 179-90). Later, as an arrogant, haughty nation, her pride causes her destruction (I, 683-88).

This presentation of France as innocent victim and responsible party arises from the nature of the concept of "Motherland." The nation is first the sum of its parts and France as a whole must bear the burden of guilt for the actions of each of the warring factions. When the poet decries haughty pride, although the context of his reproach indicates that he is addressing the Catholic nobles (I, 693-95), he reprimands France, the nation: "France, tu t'eslevois orgueilleuse" (I, 683). At the same time France is an independent entity, distinct from her component parts: as mother to the sons who murder her; as ship destroyed by its occupants. This presentation of France as both victimizer and victim captures the ambiguous position which the tragic hero occupied in Greek tragedy, touching both innocence and guilt.

The image of France as giant extends the notion of responsible victim by introducing the concept of hubris:

> Je pense encores voir un monstrueux geant,
> Qui va de braves mots les hauts cieux outrageant,
> Superbe, florissant, si brave qu'il ne treuve
> Nul qui de sa valeur entreprenne la preuve.
>
> (I, 135-38)

The giant's invincible force, which no one dares challenge, has made it a "superbe," haughty power. The very nature of its being causes its downfall, for when the giant does not encounter an opponent against whom to unleash its strength, this destructive force turns inward against itself: "Son corps est combatu, à soi-mesme contraire" (I, 141). The theme of subversive pride as the hamartia of France becomes explicit when the poet rebukes France as "orgueilleuse" (I, 683) and states that her greatness is the cause of her destruction:

> Tu as plus que jamais de merveilleuses testes,
> Des cerveaux transcendans, de vrais et faux prophetes:
> Toi, prophete, en mourant du mal de ta grandeur
> Mieux que le medecin tu chantes ton mal-heur.
>
> (I, 637-40)

Thus France as "la patrie" is responsible for her approaching demise, and yet each of the two warring factions must share the guilt individually (I, 101-102; 113; 116). The poet also implies that the civil wars, and consequently the destruction of France, are God's responsibility since He uses them to punish the stiff-necked nation. Here then, as in Greek tragedy, there exists the impenetrable realm of mysterious forces which punish man's sinful attempts to rise above the human condition. In the ancient context they were called the gods, Destiny or Fortune; within this Christian framework that power is God. Greek tragedy is characterized by the complex relationship between a sense of determinism for which the gods must be held accountable and the freedom of the hero which makes him bear the major burden of responsibility for his fate. So in *Les Tragiques,* France, as proud subject and innocent victim, shares some of her responsibility with the Calvinist God of predestination, a relationship which reflects the mystery of grace and free will.

This dual role of victimizer and victim lies at the heart of the tragic action as expressed in "Misères." From the first image of France as mother, where the fatal blows are struck from within, self-destruction is the dominant theme. The giant, as the symbol of France, is called the "meurtrier de soi-mesme" (I, 134) and the struggle of the two warring factions is described in similar terms:

> En cela le vainqueur ne demeurant plus fort,
> Que de voir son haineux le premier à la mort,
> Qu'il seconde, autochire, aussi tost de la sienne,
> Vainqueur, comme l'on peut vaincre à la Cadmeenne.
>
> (I, 187-90)

The victor, who himself has been mortally wounded in the combat, lives only long enough to see his hated victim expire; his own death follows immediately. The men born from the teeth of the dragon slain by Cadmus killed each other off and thus, in effect, murdered their brothers. By entering the battle, each combatant is responsible for killing his brother—another himself—as well as for directly causing his own death. Jean de la Taille speaks of the weapons of civil war as "teinctes en nostre propre sang," stained with the blood of one's own kin, or as the richness of poetic language allows, stained with one's own blood.[15] The theme of "meurtrier de soi-mesme" then lies at the heart of civil conflict, and reinforced in this passage by the use of "autochire," it now begins to emerge as the center of the tragic action. This interpretation is first implied by the words of the muse and is explicitly stated when the poet refers to the suicide of the giant as "la tragedie horrible" (I, 133).

This association of civil war, suicide, and dramatic tragedy was also made by Jean de la Taille, and confirms the impression that d'Aubigné knew his work well. The opening paragraph of the *Art de la tragedie,* the dedication to Henriette de Clèves, characterizes the "piteux desastres" and "la mort... si pitoyable" caused by the civil wars as subject matter proper for tragedy. Later la Taille refers explicitly to the civil wars as "les piteuses et sanglantes tragedies... jouées sur l'eschaffaut de France," describing the action in terms of suicide: "où les uns et les autres avons porté les armes teinctes en nostre propre sang."[16] Finally, to complete the relationship, la Taille considers suicide a fitting subject for tragedy, for by its very nature it moves the listener and thus fulfills tragedy's goal of "esmouvoir." All this, it would seem, is parallel and related to an interpretation of tragedy in *Les Tragiques*.

The presentation of tragic action in terms of family conflict —brother against brother, sons against their mother—recalls the type of situation Aristotle considered most capable of producing pity and fear, for it was based on the special horror with which the 4th-century Athenian considered the spilling of kindred blood and the moral stain he attached to it.[17] The ocurrence of the tragic deed within the family intensifies the affective reaction of the spectator because the hero, blinded by pride, rage, or ignorance,

---

[15] La Taille, "Dédication" to Jacques de la Taille's *Daïre,* in B. Weinberg, *Critical Prefaces of the French Renaissance* (1950), p. 234.
[16] *Ibid.,* p. 234.
[17] G. Else, *Aristotle's Poetics: The Argument* (1957), pp. 421-52.

destroys that which he loves, or that to which he is inherently bound. Or, if the deed is perpetrated consciously, in spite of family ties, then the willful perversion of the deepest natural human relationship, the denial of the most basic sentiment of the human condition, inspires the strongest feeling of fear and horror. This is not to imply that d'Aubigné knew the *Poetics* directly, for it was common to speak of the civil war in terms of intra-family strife. Both Ronsard in his *Discours des Misères de ce temps* and J. Béreau in his *Complainte de France sur la guerre civile* use this image, and Montaigne employs the same language to describe the wars in "De la physionomie." The essayist characterizes the conflict in terms of self-destruction reminiscent of the image of the giant; he also speaks of the civil strife as "haines parricides" and as the dismemberment of "sa mere."[18] He sees himself as a spectator to the dramatic representation of suicide which, because it evokes his "desplaisir" as well as his "plaisir," he likens to the experience of tragedy.[19] Like la Taille, and like d'Aubigné, Montaigne has felt an inherent relationship among civil war, suicide, and dramatic tragedy.

The tragedy of France has relentlessly followed its fatal course toward the destruction of the hero because of the unwillingness of certain elements to see and to act. The poet does not specifically characterize France as blind, but as the victim of pride which has concealed the true nature of her self and her action; it is evident that blindness is one of her distinctive faults. Like the proud Oedipus, she is ironically working toward her own destruction. More specifically, however, France is blind because so many of her leaders and citizens are blind. The poet reproaches the judges and bankers who in their pride oppress the weak and the poor, failing to recognize the tragedy in which they have been taking part. Blind to reality, they have stood as spectators as if removed from the context of the dramatic action. The poet's cry is "See! wake up from your blindness, realize that you too are embarked on this ship which is sinking":

> Car encor vous pourriez contempler de bien loin
> Une nef sans pouvoir luy aider...

---

[18] Montaigne, *Les Essais*, ed. Villey (1923), III, 12, p. 346.
[19] *Ibid.*, p. 353.

> Mais quand, dedans la mer, la mer pareillement
> Vous menace de mort, courez à la tempeste,
> Car avec le vaisseau vostre ruine est preste.
>
> (I, 171-78)

D'Aubigné here comes close to the modern reading of Aristotle that in tragedy the spectator is to identify with the tragic character, for on this feeling for one "like himself" depends his experience of fear and pity.[20] This was not a notion discussed in the 16th-century theories of tragedy and it is interesting that d'Aubigné in his own way arrived at it himself. The poet's own response to the suffering of the tragic hero—his realization of the tragedy in which he too is involved—is the composition of *Les Tragiques*.

II

Until the present time, the poet has been among those who ignored the civil strife threatening the very existence of France:

> Quand j'estois fol heureux, si cet heur est folie
> De rire ayant sur soi sa maison demolie,
> Si c'est heur d'appliquer son fol entendement
> Au doux laissant l'utile, estre sans sentiment
> Lepreux de la cervelle, et rire des miseres
> Qui accablent le col du païs et des freres,
> Je fleurissois comm'eux de ces mesmes propos,
> Quand par l'oisiveté je perdois le repos.
>
> (II, 69-76)

Now he reproaches himself for having written love poetry, characterizing his mind as diseased—"lepreux de la cervelle"—for giving himself to the "doux," to what he considered happiness. Unaware of his own situation, "sans sentiment," and thus blind to the world about, he turned his back on the suffering and misery of his "brothers" and laughed and played in its presence. The repetition of "fol" and "folie" emphasizes the false nature of his "heur," expressing perhaps a sense of the etymological relationship of "fol" to "follis" (a puffed up bag or balloon, a swollen void).

---

[20] Else, *op. cit.*, p. 436.

Like the bankers and judges, he has remained outside the action, an unmoved spectator to tragedy. Now the poet turns from his "oisiveté" and useless poetry. Inspired by God to see truth and no longer afraid of the consequences of what he might say, he recognizes the real nature of the world in which he lives and accepts the role he must play (II, 43-44). He acknowledges the light of truth which he refused to see before: "combien de fois fermee / Ai-je à la verité la lumiere allumee?" (II, 21-22).

The opening verses of *Les Tragiques* promise forceful personal action as the poet sets out to "s'attacquer aux legions de Rome / Aux monstres d'Italie" (I, 1-2). He scoffs at the caution, fear and doubt which made Caesar hesitate at the Rubicon and compares himself to Hannibal, "qui...se fendit un passage aux Alpes embrasez" (I, 4): he too is going to "brise(r) les rochers" (I, 7) and "(faire) breche au lieu de porte" (I, 6). The poet's task will be the "delivrance" (I, 15) of the captive Church and he calls upon God to "fendre" (I, 36) the hardened hearts of those who refuse His word. Yet this promise of action is not fulfilled in "Misères"; the verbs which characterize the poet's role in this first book are the more passive ones of depicting, portraying. He speaks of his subject matter as "(le) general discours / De mon tableau public" (I, 367); as a "portraict... de la France" (I, 424); as the "tableau de l'Eglise" (I, 1341). In itself this descriptive narrative of the tragic state of affairs in France represents the first significant act of the poet after becoming aware of the truth. No longer an oblivious onlooker, but an interested spectator, profoundly concerned with the future course of the tragedy, he has sought to recapitulate past events, to understand their import, and to situate them in relation to himself and the reader before attempting vigorous and meaningful action.

From the opening verses of "Princes," the poet has assumed a new function. With the shafts of "la vive lumiere" as his weapon, he is going to "crever l'enflé Pithon" (II, 2), "percer... les pestes et les roignes" (II, 5), "ouvrir les fonds hideux" (II, 6). The tyrannical giant of evil who is his enemy will be slain by the sling of truth, with the poem as its stone:

> L'ennemi mourra donc, puisque la peur est morte.
> Le temps a creü le mal; je viens en cette sorte,
> Croissant avec le temps de style, de fureur,
> D'aage, de volonté, d'entreprise et de cœur;

> Car d'autant que le monde est roide en sa malice,
> Je deviens roide aussi pour guerroyer le vice.
>
> (II, 49-54)

The attack on the legions of Rome and the monsters of Italy in the battle to free the captive Church has evidently begun, for the poet has moved from spectator to participant in the action:

> La main peut s'endormir, non l'ame reposer,
> Et voir en mesme temps nostre mere hardie
> Sur ses costez jouër si dure tragedie,
> Proche à sa catastrophe, où tant d'actes passez
> Me font frapper des mains et dire: c'est assez!
>
> (II, 80-84)

He now realizes that so many acts of the tragedy have already passed that the catastrophe, the fatal climax, is near. The active hand might not take part in the struggle, but once the true nature of the times has been discovered, the sensitive, cognitive "âme" can no longer turn from reality. The poet here indicates that he is going to combine the two actions. By clapping his hands and shouting "enough" he arrests the movement of the tragic course of events and moves into the action as a lucid, physically active character whose efforts will strive to effect a reversal of fortune which results in the salvation of "nostre mere hardie." The tragic prologue has ended and the actual dramatic tragedy of *Les Tragiques* has begun: the poet has become actor, the reader has become spectator, and the tragic action now begins to unfold before our very eyes.

III

The image of "nostre mere hardie" supports the designation of France, the mother, as the tragic hero of the narrative prologue of "Misères." Yet the opening verses of the poem promised the deliverance of the Protestant Church. The portrait of "la mi-morte France" (I, 885) presented in the first thousand or so lines of "Misères" is, in fact, paralleled by the "tableau de l'Eglise" (I, 1341), with which the first book ends. Like the situation of France in the tragedy of the civil wars, the position of the Church is characterized by the reversal of natural order: the enemies of God, rather than His people, reign supreme on earth. [21] The focus changes from a lament on the death of France to the destruction of the true Protestant Church; the same events which are first viewed in social and political terms are now interpreted with regard to the religious conflict between Protestants and Catholics. The prayer with which "Misères" ends is a Protestant supplication to God for vengeance, and the "misères" of which it speaks are those of the persecuted Huguenots: "Soyent tes yeux adoucis à guerir nos miseres" (I, 1353).

This shift from the social and political to the religious is carried through the image of "mère." The analogous presentation of the two portraits would suggest this although the Church is not specifically referred to as a mother. In this same prayer, it is pictured as a woman in chains: "les fers aux pieds, sur les geennes assise, / A sa gorge la corde et le fer inhumain" (I, 1342-43). She too is innocent, yet guilty of pride, and certainly under the altar of the idols where the poet sees her "visage meurtri" (I, 14), she appears "proche à sa catastrophe." Thus the "mere hardie" whom the poet will attempt to save symbolizes the Protestant Church as well as France. From this point on, the religious situation dominates. The tragedy of France becomes an integral part of the greater struggle in which the Protestant Church is engaged. The theme of national disorder moves into the background, to appear from time to time throughout the work. It has served its primary purpose by providing the framework against which the situation of the Church has emerged as tragedy. [22]

The antagonists in the terrestrial realm of the drama are the Catholic princes and judges against whom the poet sustains his

---

[21] D'Aubigné characterizes the situation caused by the civil war as a "monde à l'envers," "Misères," verse 235.

[22] The concept of the universe as a theater in which history is played out was not peculiar to d'Aubigné. Calvin envisioned the world as a stage on which human history unfolded as scenes in a drama, with God and the angels as spectators and actors, and the Protestant Church as protagonist: "Sed satis est coram Deo et angelis totoque piorum theatro benedictam esse eorum memoriam." *Corpus Reformatorum*, XXXII, p. 175; "Debent igitur ac si in celeberrimo theatro essent vivere; quia sub conspectu Dei et angelorum vivunt." *CR*, L, p. 220. See also the *Institutes*, I, v, 5; I, vi, 2; I, xiv, 20; II, v, 1.

attack through "Princes" and "Chambre Dorée"; they are directly and immediately responsible for the massacre of the Protestants and the destruction of the Church. In both cases, they have reacted to the horror and carnage they have created by blinding themselves to this reality:

> Deschaussons le cothurne et rions, car il faut
> Jetter ce sang tout frais hors de nostre eschaffaut,
> En prodiguant dessus mille fleurs espanchees,
> Pour cacher nostre meurtre à l'ombre des jonchees.
> (II, 211-14)

On the stage of France where the tragedy is being played out, the kings desire to remove the cothurni they wear to end the drama, not as the poet has done by recognizing and attempting actively to change things, but by avoiding truth. They are going to conceal the blood of their murdered victims by bedecking the stage-death scaffold with flowers, and by replacing the tragedy with comedy, escaping through farces and games: "Quand ce siecle n'est rien qu'une histoire tragique, / Ce sont farces et jeux toutes leurs actions" (II, 206-207). But real tragedy, where "la mort jouë elle-mesme," does not end when the antagonists take off the buskins. The events portrayed on the stage have taken place and the flowers must wither and die, revealing once again the tragic posture of the Church.

The guilt of these active persecutors is shared through complicity by all Catholics who are a party to these deeds. Scenes of massacre described by autos-da-fé in Spain present the tragedy of the Church in Europe in microcosmic form:

> L'Europe se monstra: Dieu vid sa contenance
> Fumeuse par les feux esmeus sur l'innocence,
> Vid les publiques lieux, les palais les plus beaux
> Pleins de peuples bruyans, qui pour les jeux nouveaux
> Estaloyent à la mort les plus entieres vies
> En spectacles plaisans et feintes tragedies...
>   ...Là, de mesme maniere
> Qu'aux theatres on vid s'eschauffer les Romains,
> Ce peuple desbauché applaudissoit des mains.
> (III, 613-24)

The very setting reveals the dramatic nature of the tragic scene, reinforcing an earlier reference to the platform containing the victims as "eschaffaut" (III, 545). These innocent victims are the protagonists in this "spectacle," with the executioners—Catholic priests and royalty—as the antagonists. In the presence of these deaths being played out before their very eyes, the zealous Catholics, animated by "faux zele d'erreur," sit as spectators. They signify their approval by their heated applause and thus become accomplices to the crime. Like their spiritual and political leaders, they remain blind to the tragedy. What they see is a "spectacle plaisan," a "jeu nouveau," similar to a farce, a ballet, or a comedy which diverts and amuses. The "tragedies" are "feintes," unreal or played, because not seen as tragedy. They cheer the "heretics'" destruction, remaining cold, distant, and unmoved by what they see.

The truth is, the poet reveals, that these Catholics have themselves revolted against God (II, 457-58). The title originally given to "Chambre Dorée," where scenes like the auto-da-fé abound, was "Ubris"; d'Aubigné made the change, as he says, "aimant mieux que tout parlast françois." [23] The chariot of Themis—the goddess of justice—is depicted rolling over the bodies of the iniquitous, "des monstres avortez par l'infidelle Ubris" (III, 892). The Catholics are guilty of insolent pride, engendered by Até, divine malediction. Like the Pope in "Misères" (1235-44), they do not seek to fulfill God's will, but desire to impose their own plan on the world's destiny. Blindly they exceed the limits imposed on them by the human condition and thus unwittingly pursue their own destruction. This description of the downfall of the Catholics, and the implication that their crimes result in part from a divine curse, suggest that they, as tragic antagonists, become the real tragic victims once the course of the action has been changed. This judgment must be reserved until the end of the drama, for here the poet manifests no sympathy for them as victims, vilifying them as cannibals, serpents and butchers. The allegorical vices which inhabit the Palais de Justice personify the evils which possess them, preventing any spectator from experiencing pity. The victims in this drama remain the Protestant martyrs, for the poet characterizes their deaths as tragedies (III, 582). The murder of each innocent Huguenot is a tragedy which reflects that of the "Eglise," for the faithful are the Church. This

---

[23] D'Aubigné, "Aux lecteurs," in *Les Tragiques*, ed. Garnier et Plattard (1932), p. 11.

equation of the part and the whole is manifested by the juxtaposition of the portrait in "Misères" of the "visage de la captive Eglise" (14) under the altars of the idols to the presentation in the Revelation of St. John which presents the individual souls of the martyrs. The death of each of the faithful foreshadows the death of the Church; each death means that a little more of the "Eglise" has died.

As the drama is played out on the stage of the terrestrial universe, the Elect in Heaven view the action from their spiritual vantage point. Virtue describes their perspective as she attempts to lead the young man in God's way:

> Je veux faire voller ton esprit sur la nuë,
> Que tu voye la terre en ce poinct que la vid
> Scipion quand l'amour de mon nom le ravit,
> Ou mieux d'où Coligni se rioit de la foulle
> Qui de son tronc roullé se joüoit à la boulle,
> Parmi si hauts plaisirs que, mesme en lieu si doux,
> De tout ce qu'il voyoit il n'entroit en courroux.
> Un jeu lui fut des Rois la sotte perfidie,
> Comique le succez de la grand' tragedie.
>
> (II, 1428-36)

The reference to Scipio and its juxtaposition with Coligny serves to elucidate the Admiral's perspective, providing, at this early point in the poem, an essential view of the action of the tragedy. Scipio's dream, as recorded by Cicero in *De Re Publica* tells of Scipio's ascent to Heaven in a dream.[24] From this vantage point he saw the world as it is—a small and inconsequential part of the total universe —and he recognized the paltriness of human endeavor and achievement. In the light of this discovery, Scipio turned from the empty values which man esteems to the substantial and eternal heavenly virtues, as he was advised to do:

> I see that you are still directing your gaze upon
> the habitation and abode of men. If it seems
> small to you, as it actually is, keep your gaze
> fixed upon these heavenly things, and scorn the

---

[24] Cicero, *De Re Publica*, trans. by C. W. Keyes, Loeb Classical Library (1943), pp. 261-83.

> earthly. For what fame can you gain from the
> speech of men, or what glory that is worth seeking. [25]

These insights characterize Coligny's position, for the Admiral too has ascended to Heaven (although his ascent takes place after his death). He too sees terrestrial activity in its proper perspective. What is happening in France, as what happened in Rome, is only a small part of what is happening in the world, and the world is only an infinitesimal point in the universe: "Là ne s'estime rien des regnes l'excellence, / Le monde n'est qu'un poix, un atome la France" (II, 1439-40). The duration of life on earth, its fame and fortune, mean so little in the presence of eternity.

Scipio's dream also predicts his future success and by analogy serves to disclose the future course of the action of *Les Tragiques*: the eventual triumph of Coligny and his Protestant cause. This parallel is reinforced by the similarity of the lives of Scipio and Coligny—military hero, statesman of influence, man of virtue, honor and wisdom who sought national unity, and who met death at the hands of political enemies—and by the reasons given for Scipio's salvation: patriotism and virtue. The elder Scipio Africanus praises his son's concern for the fatherland, advising him of the eternal afterlife of happiness which awaits the patriot:

> All those who have preserved, aided or enlarged
> the fatherland have a special place prepared for
> them in the heavens, where they may enjoy an
> eternal afterlife of happiness. [26]

Coligny too has been a patriot, and the guarantee of salvation has already been fulfilled; its realization awaits his spiritual and political heirs. Prominent among these is the poet himself, attempting to save France through his poem.

The elder Africanus indicates that the second means to salvation lies in the practice of virtue, in the love of justice and duty:

---

[25] *Ibid.*, p. 273: Sentio, inquit, te sedem etiam nunc hominum ac domum contemplari; quae si tibi parva, ut est, ita videtur, haec caelestia semper spectato, illa humana contemnito. tu enim quam celebritatem sermonis hominum aut quam expetendam consequi gloriam potes. (VI, 20)

[26] *Ibid.*, p. 265: Omnibus, qui patriam conservaverint, adiuverint, auxerint, certum esse in caelo definitum locum, ubi beati aevo sempiterno fruantur. (VI, 13)

Love justice and duty, which are indeed strictly due to parents and kinsmen but most of all to the fatherland. Such a life is the road to the skies. [27]

In "Princes," Virtue herself has been offering Coligny as a model to be emulated, for his ideals of justice, duty, and moral excellence have led him to Heaven. In d'Aubigné's view of the religious struggle, these values are intimately associated with the Protestant cause as a whole. [28] This again indicates ultimate success for the poet and his people, foreshadowing the felicitous dénouement—the "comique succez"— of the tragic action of *Les Tragiques*.

The intellectual and spiritual distance of this heavenly perspective separates Coligny and the Elect from the action and makes them the first real spectators to the drama. From this vantage point, the Catholic bankers and judges, and the zealots present at the autos-da-fé are only spectators to a play within a play. They are the audience at a spectacle which is at the same time a microcosmic reflection of the larger universal drama and a small scene in it. These "spectators" participate in the action of the tragedy of the Church; they are actors, passive characters who encourage and incite the active villains, and share their guilt. Ironically, although for obviously different reasons, Coligny experiences the same lack of concern for the apparently disastrous course of the tragic action. As he stands in Heaven, looking down on the world, he cannot appreciate the urgent position of the Church as the "fall of a great hero." He is aware that in spite of current appearances, the Church and her people will be saved, and her enemies damned. Realizing the insignificance of all man's endeavors, and fully cognizant that human destiny is determined by God's will, Coligny must think of the "succez"—the progress or outcome—of the "grand tragedie" as "comique." From the celestial vantage point, the Admiral is a spectator to a dramatic comedy: the characters are of lower station than the Elect; their actions are inconsequential in the framework of the universe; the essential action progresses from misery on earth to eternal happiness in Heaven; the emotional response is not pity or fear but elation.

---

[27] *Ibid.*, p. 269: Justitiam cole et pietatem, quae cum magna in parentibus et propinquis, tum in patria maxima est; ea vita est in caelum. (VI, 16)
[28] Sauerwein, *op. cit.*, pp. 93-96.

Why then is the poem not called *Les Comiques*? The answer lies in the fact that the poet, and not Coligny, provides the focus from which the events of the drama are interpreted. From the finite terrestrial perspective of the human mind and soul with which he sees and understands, the poet recognized the impending ruin of his country and his Church, and the self-annihilation of his compatriots and coreligionists. This horrible destruction of something greater than he, falling because of pride and divine anger, aroused his compassion and fear, and he characterized it as tragedy. A divine light does make him aware of the true nature of the situation. His soul, "furieuse de sainct amour" ("Préface," 132), has been mystically drawn to God and his "cœur" —as much will as heart— has been possessed by Truth ("Préface," 145-46). Divine inspiration, growing in frequency and intensity as the poem progresses, allows him to share the celestial perspective. Although the focus of "Princes" and "Chambre Dorée" is an essentially terrestrial one, the poet's function through the rest of *Les Tragiques* is the gradual reinterpretation of the earthly "tragedy" from Coligny's point of view, until the felicitous dénouement of the original drama is finally accomplished. He comes indeed to appreciate the significance of worldly events as Coligny does. But he rarely attains the Admiral's emotional peace. He himself is careful to emphasize that his state of divine inspiration exists only "quelquesfois" ("Préface," 355); the poem in general is written under God's guidance, but only at times does the human soul rise as high as the heavenly heights. Thus even when revealing the overwhelming positive value of martyrdom he still speaks with hatred and rage of the executioners. Despite the elevated vantage point he reaches, the poet essentially remains an actor in the drama and cannot distance himself emotionally from the events; as a man, he experiences human reactions. Speaking of the cruel deaths of innocent children, he cries out in anguish: "Mais quel crime avant vivre ont-ils peu encourir?" (V, 619). This question, raised to God, is asked by a man at that time unmindful of the celestial significance of terrestrial events. From this point of view, he characterizes the voices of the victims in "Fers" as "tragiques voix" (V, 615), the civil conflict in that same book as "tragiques erreurs" (V, 366), and the battle of Moncontour as a "tragique bataille" (V, 420). This tension between the poet's two perspectives continues to the end of the poem when it is finally resolved in his assumption into Heaven. Then the poet takes his place for all eternity "au giron de son Dieu" alongside Coligny and the Elect.

The presentation of the St. Bartholomew's Day massacre reflects the dual nature of this perspective. Present in Heaven as the Elect view the paintings and the prose gloss which reveal the true meaning of the massacre, the poet records what he sees and reads. He also copies the comments of Coligny, which disclose the perfidy of the Catholics as well as the pride of the Protestants, and which acknowledge the hardship which God's punishment of this pride has wrought. In the Admiral's eyes, God has remained faithful to his disloyal children by using this suffering to lead them to salvation. This is then the meaning which the poet communicates, but in spite of his exalted vantage point he retains his human emotional reaction. He characterizes what he sees as "la tragedie qui efface le reste" (V, 702), like the auto-da-fé, a microcosm of the great tragedy of the Church. Dawn, he says,

> ...tire en tremblant du monde le rideau,
> Et le soleil voyant le spectacle nouveau
> A regret esleva son pasle front des ondes.
>
> (V, 779-81)

The murder of Jeanne d'Albret represented the first act of this play within a play: "le coup de poison qui de la tragedie/ Joüa l'acte premier" (V, 753-54). At the same time, the descriptive terms of light and brightness which frame the presentation of these "tableaux," directly reflect the essential positive value which God gives to these events. What has been characterized as "tragedies" is presented in these terms:

> Le paradis plus beau de spectacles si beaux
> Aima le parement de tels sacrés tableaux,
> Si que du vif esclat de couleurs immortelles
> Les voutes du beau ciel reluisirent plus belles.
>
> (V, 273-76)

The Elect themselves are attracted to the painting of Jeanne's funeral by its brilliance:

> Jà les vives splendeurs des diversités peintes
> Tiroyent, à l'approcher, les yeux des ames sainctes...
> L'esclatante lueur prés de l'œil accroissoit.
>
> (V, 745-48)

While Coligny watches the suffering of the innocent in a detached manner, God shares the poet's bitterness as He rages against injustice and weeps for His children:

> Dieu voulut en voir plus, mais de regret et d'ire
> Tout son sang escuma: il fuit, il se retire,
> Met ses mains au devant de ses yeux en courroux.
> Le Tout-Puissant ne peut resider entre nous.
> Sa barbe et ses cheveux de fureur herisserent,
> Les sourcis de son front en rides s'enfoncerent,
> Ses yeux changés en feu jetterent pleurs amers.
>
> (IV, 1389-95)

Yet God knows of the salvation that awaits the righteous and of the damnation promised to the wicked, for He has determined it since the beginning of time. Two factors appear to determine God's role. First, unlike the Elect who play no part in the drama, God is an active participant in the action. On the terrestrial level, His force sustains the martyrs, giving them the strength by which they endure the painful path to salvation: "Cette constance extreme.../Vient de Dieu...present au milieu de vos flammes" (IV, 1353-58). On the spiritual level of the action, where Satan and the black angels join the Catholic iniquitous against the Heavenly hosts and the just Protestants on earth, God is the active commander of the forces of good: "...ce grand Chef souverain, / Commande de la voix et combat de sa main" (IV, 1359-60). God is a spectator who watches the individual incidents and the course of events with great interest. But because He is the chief protagonist as well, He does not always maintain an emotional distance.

The other attribute of God, on which the first really depends, is the anthropomorphic quality of the Divine Being. This is not the God incarnate of the New Testament. The poem, in fact, assigns a conspicuously small role to Christ. The God of *Les Tragiques* is the God of the Old Testament who actively punished His people in His anger and grief and shared their triumphs in His joy. The many references in the poem to Old Testament events and the continuing analogy between the Protestants and the Hebrews as the chosen people play a major part in creating the Old Testament atmosphere of the poem. Since He is spiritually and physically involved in the individual and collective destiny of His children, God shares their joy and sorrow, becomes angry in the face of evil and weeps when the innocent suffer. The Elect in Heaven devote themselves wholly to the contemplation of divine glory and no longer experience "passion charnelle" (V, 289). The anthropomorphic God who participates in the action does.

IV

After the prologue of "Misères," the dramatic tragedy of *Les Tragiques* is divided into two parts. The next four books —"Princes," "Chambre Dorée," "Feux," and "Fers"— represent the battle between the spiritual and terrestrial forces of good and evil. From his vantage point in Heaven, the poet fulfills his role as active participant by relating the activities of the characters and revealing the true significance of events, thus allowing the felicitous dénouement. He describes the personal contest between God and Satan, the roles played by the celestial angels and the fallen followers of the Devil, and human conflicts of all magnitudes, from great military encounters to individual martyrdom. By the last two books, "Vengeances" and "Jugement," these conflicts have been resolved and only the punishment of the wicked and the reward of the just remain.[29] It is in the resolution of the dramatic action that the poet assumes a more active role. In "Vengeances," he becomes the prophet of God, and is assimilated to Jonah by three analogous circumstances. First, they share an initial unwillingness to answer God's call: "Je m'enfuyois de Dieu" (VI, 115). Second, both have subsequently been awakened by God: "Le doigt de Dieu me leve et l'ame encore vive / M'anime à guerroyer la puante Ninive" (VI, 137-38); and third, both are prophets of doom, carrying messages of forthcoming destruction. As Jonah came to warn ancient Nineveh, the poet comes to destroy its modern counterpart, Paris. The words he is presenting are comparable to the words of Scripture: "Ainsi les visions qui seront ici peintes / Seront exemples vrais de nos histoires sainctes" (VI, 89-90). As God revealed His word in Scripture through the prophet, so it is revealed in *Les Tragiques*.

With the coming of the time of final judgment in "Jugement," the poet moves even closer to God as he and his poem become the

---

[29] *Ibid.*, pp. 148-172.

actual instrument by which ultimate justice is carried out: "Pour me faire instrument à ces effects divers, / Donne force à ma voix, efficace à mes vers" (VII, 7-8). Through the verse itself, eternal happiness and damnation are accomplished. This must be taken literally, for the poet announces who is to be saved and who damned: "A celui qui t'avouë, ou bien qui te renonce, / Porte l'heur ou malheur, l'arrest que je prononce" (VII, 9-10). The poet possesses what he calls "ce pacquet à malheurs ou de parfaicte joye" (VII, 22), which, when opened, separates the Elect from the multitude. God and the poet alone are the active protagonists as the rest of the universe waits passively to be chosen for Heaven or Hell. When his role has been fulfilled and the course of events of the original tragedy successfully resolved, the poet receives the reward promised by the dream of Scipio. The curtain falls as he is assumed into Heaven, to enjoy the eternal glory of the celestial afterlife.

V

The question posed earlier as to who is meant by the title *Les Tragiques* can now be discussed. The Protestant protagonists lay strong claim to the title of "the tragic ones." The situation of France which defines the tragic action has given way to the religious context where the Protestant Church becomes the "mere hardie" at the point of catastrophe. Because the Church and its followers are the chosen people, their downfall caused by an excess of pride and weakening faith exemplifies the fall of a great hero through an error in judgment. In their blindness they have been working toward their own demise. In time, however, and with divine sanction, their reversal of fortune leads to a felicitous dénouement. The author has succeeded in maintaining that dual perspective characteristic of Greek tragedy whereby both the human viewpoint which admires heroic nobility and innocence and the divine which recognizes sin and guilt are sustained through the work. As the poet moves between his terrestrial and celestial vantage points, the picture of the Protestants as both guilty and innocent emerges. The audience, which would find the downfall of a totally virtuous hero repugnant and horrible, can thus feel pity for his suffering. In Aristotelian terms as d'Aubigné might have understood them, and with allowances made for the epic context which permits the hero to be something other than a man, the Protestant Church and its people qualify as the "tragiques." This view is confirmed by the fact that every reference to "tragiques" and "tragédie" used in a religious context refers to the Protestants.

The resemblance of *Les Tragiques* to André de Rivaudeau's *Aman* also supports this view. The analogy in the poem between the Calvinist Protestants and the Hebrews is well established and applies as well to the Hebrews of *Aman*. Rivaudeau's religious intention was to portray Aman's victims as the heroes of his drama; his sympathy went out to the spiritual ancestors of his people and he sought to inform and encourage his coreligionists by their example.

The comparison with *Aman* also reveals a similarity between the character and destiny of Aman and that of the Catholic antagonists of *Les Tragiques*. In Rivaudeau's tragedy, the iniquitous chamberlain is the moving force of the action and the course of his career —pride, revolt against the gods, reversal of fortune, downfall, and death— represents the stages of the dramatic complication and dénouement. Until the entrance of the poet into the action, the Catholics occupy the same role as their wicked predecessor. This presentation ironically allows these villains to appear as satanic heroes. Although Aman is all bad, and thus cannot evoke pity, his counterparts in the poem seem not to be totally wicked. In "Jugement," the poet suggests that the iniquitous may repent and change their ways, thus achieving salvation:

> Doncques chacun de vous, pauvres payens...
> Suyvez, aimez Sara, si vous avez dessein
> D'estre fils d'Abraham, retirés en son sein.
>   (VII, 631-46)

If the souls of the wicked are always redeemable, then the propensity for good exists in them. Thus, in essence, they are not totally bad, but are perhaps lost sheep, God's children who have gone astray. Their damnation, which results from their denial of this latent good in themselves, can therefore represent a tragedy, the loss of a potentially good soul.

The resolution of the problem of who are *Les Tragiques* lies in the realization that neither the Protestants nor the Catholics alone are implied by this title. The action of the drama describes the simultaneous peripeteias of both parties whereby the initial victim becomes the triumphant hero while the original victor becomes the ultimate victim. The Calvinist context of the poem resolves the problem of the hero in favor of the Protestants. From the poet's human point of view, his coreligionists and his Church are heroic victims of a dread tragedy; the apparent disproportion between their crime and their fate provokes his anger and pity. From his celestial viewpoint, the Huguenots appear as the heroes of a felicitous tragedy; here, their just destiny elicits his admiration and his joy. The Catholics in both instances represent the iniquitous forces of evil whose deserved punishment evokes his satisfaction. The suggestion that they are "lost souls" does, however, allow a reaction of tempered pity, and derives wholly from the celestial perspective. Thus the Protestants partake of the name "tragic ones" as heroes, and the Catholics as victims.

CHAPTER III

PROTESTANT APOCALYPSE

I

Recent studies on *Les Tragiques* have tended to bear out Jean Trénel's assertion in 1904 that d'Aubigné is "le plus biblique des écrivains français." [1] Since Trénel's catalogue of Scriptural references and Hebraisms in the poem (by which he sought to prove his point), critics have given more thought to the significance of this accumulation of Biblical imagery, focusing particularly on d'Aubigné's continuing correlation of characters and events in Old Testament, early Christian, and contemporary sixteenth-century history. Henri Weber, whose view represents the most generally accepted interpretation, explains that this correlation provides the temporal dimension required by the epic poem. Moreover, by showing contemporary events to be a repetition of Biblical history, it raises those events to a symbolic level consistent with d'Aubigné's notion that the fortunes of the Protestants represent the working out of God's providential design for His modern-day chosen people. [2] Henry Sauerwein suggests that the Biblical imagery represents the poet's attempt to approximate the style of the Bible in order to achieve a form suited to *Les Tragiques* as God's revelation of the destiny of the Protestant people to the divinely inspired author. [3]

---

[1] Jean Trénel, *L'Elément biblique dans l'œuvre poétique d'Agrippa d'Aubigné* (1904), p. 1.
[2] Henri Weber, *La Création poétique au XVIe siècle en France de Maurice Scève à Agrippa d'Aubigné* (1956), pp. 605-608; See also J. A. Walker, "D'Aubigné's *Les Tragiques*: A Genre Study," *UTQ*, xxxiii (1964), 109-124.
[3] Henry Sauerwein, *Agrippa d'Aubigné's Les Tragiques* (1953), pp. 173-212.

D'Aubigné's reliance on Scripture is not surprising since, as a Calvinist, he believed that the Bible represented the only source of Divine revelation. Moreover, through grace and faith, man might attain limited insight into its meaning; here might be found the key to the significance of contemporary history. The juxtaposition of a Biblical event related and commented on by God or a divine agent with an event from current history could suggest the divine purpose of the modern situation to the discerning eye of the elect. D'Aubigné appears to have chosen his images at random —more often from the Old Testament than from the New— wherever he apparently perceived a meaningful analogy with his own times. In one case, however, there is an important parallel, which has gone virtually unnoticed, with a particular book of the Bible — St. John's Book of Revelation. Certain critics, including Sauerwein, Imbrie Buffum, Jean Plattard, and particularly Henri Weber, have indicated the "apocalyptic" nature of certain passages which describe the destruction of the world, especially those in "Jugement."[4] Only Samuel Rocheblave, in his biography of d'Aubigné published in 1910, and in the 1930 Edition du Centenaire, touches directly on the relationship between *Les Tragiques* and the Book of Revelation, but this insight is an impressionistic one, unsupported by textual evidence.[5] Our first effort will be to substantiate that relationship; its centrality will emerge by relating it to the understanding of *Les Tragiques* as d'Aubigné's response to the world in which he lived.

The cosmological drama of *Les Tragiques* is presented in terms which correspond to those in John's symbolic vision in Revelation. The repeated plea for vengeance of the persecuted Protestants, "ames dessous l'autel victimes des idoles" ("Feux," l. 53), echoes the cry for revenge of the martyred souls under the altar whom John beholds when the fifth seal of the scroll is opened (vi. 9-11). The clamor for the "vendange" of divine retribution in "Princes" (l. 1514)

---

[4] Sauerwein, p. 136; Imbrie Buffum, *Agrippa d'Aubigné's Les Tragiques* (1951), pp. 62-63; Jean Plattard, *Une figure de premier plan dans nos lettres de la Renaissance: Agrippa d'Aubigné* (1931), pp. 63-67; Weber, p. 732. See also Robert Griffen, "The Rebirth Motive in Agrippa d'Aubigné's *Le Printemps*," *French Studies*, xix (1965), pp. 227-238, for apocalyptic notes in *Le Printemps*.

[5] *Agrippa d'Aubigné* (1910), p. 82; Edition du Centenaire (1930), pp. 162-63.

recalls the language of John's description of final judgment as the harvest of the grapes (xiv. 18), and the prayer for justice in "Chambre Dorée" takes the same form used by the Spirit and his bride to call the Elect to them in Revelation:

> "Vien, dit l'esprit, acours pour defendre le tien."
> "Vien," dit l'espouse, et nous avec l'espouse: "Vien!"
>
> (ll. 1061-62)
>
> Et spiritus et sponsa dicunt: Veni. Et qui audit dicat: Veni.
>
> (xxii. 17)[6]

The multitude of the Elect in d'Aubigné's presentation of Heaven corresponds to the chosen souls whom John sees after the opening of the sixth seal (vii. 1-12); they too, predestined for salvation since the beginning of the world ("Feux," l. 10), have been cleansed and made worthy of eternal life through the sacrifice of Christ, the Lamb ("Misères," l. 1260). Clothed in white robes, the Elect of both visions render praise to their God ("Feux," l. 6).

The Roman Catholic Church and its followers who persecute d'Aubigné's coreligionists are called Babylon ("Misères," l. 1302), the whore in Revelation who symbolizes all the abominations of the earth (xvii-xviii). The leader of this party, and the most tenacious tormentor of the true Church, the Pope, is represented by epithets ("Misères," l. 1213; "Jugement," l. 839) which refer in Revelation to the beast who fights with the Lamb (xvii. 12-14) and to Apollyon, the king of the abyss (ix. 11). The agents of this king who torment the Elect on earth appear as locusts in Revelation (ix. 6-12); in d'Aubigné's mind they correspond to the Catholic priests whom he calls "les puantes chenilles" which have appeared "du grand puits infernal" ("Fers," l. 448). The poet turns to Revelation again (xii. 13-18) to present the Evangelical Church as a pregnant woman forced to flee into the desert to escape her oppressors ("Vengeances," l. 150). Divine vengeance and the reordering of this spiritual disorder is promised by the poem at a time characterized by the number 666 ("Fers," l. 1416); Revelation calls this the "numerum bestiae" (xiii. 18).

---

[6] Biblical quotations are taken from the Tremellius *Biblia Sacra* (1579) and are referred to by chapter and verse.

D'Aubigné's poetic descriptions of the final destruction of the wicked thus resemble the annihilation of God's enemies in Revelation because they represent the necessary, corresponding dénouement of the analogous conflicts described in *Les Tragiques* and John's vision. The hail, brimstone, and fire which rain down upon the earth as divine retribution at the end of "Vengeances" (l. 1123) recall a similar description in the Book of Revelation (iv. 18). In order to describe the events which precede the end of time, d'Aubigné paraphrases and develops the catastrophic results of the opening of the sixth seal (vi. 12-17):

> Ce que le monde a veu d'effroyables orages,
> De gouffres caverneux, et de monts de nuages,
> De double obscurité, dont, au profond milieu,
> Le plus creux vomissoit des aiguillons de feu,
> Tout ce qu'au front du ciel on vid onc de coleres
> Estoit serenité...
> Voici la mort du ciel en l'effort douloureux
> Qui lui noircit la bouche et fait saigner les yeux...
> Le soleil vest de noir le bel or de ses feux,
> Le bel œil de ce monde est privé de ses yeux...
> La lune perd l'argent de son teint clair et blanc...
> Toute estoile se meurt...
> Tout se cache de peur...
>
> ("Jugement," ll. 903-29)

Et ecce terraemotus magnus factus est: et sol factus est niger ut saccus cilicinus, et luna tota facta est ut sanguis: Et stellae coeli ceciderunt in terram. ... Et reges terrae ... et potentes, omnesque tum servi tum ingenui absconderunt se ... Nam venit dies ille magnus irae illius: et qui poterit stare?

The first of these so-called "apocalyptic" passages appears in "Chambre Dorée," long before the actual punishment of the iniquitous is carried out. God descends to earth in response to the prayers and tears of His persecuted faithful, accompanied by terrestrial upheaval reminiscent of the devastation caused by the seventh bowl of the wrath of God in Revelation:

> ... à l'esclair de ses yeux
> Les cieux se sont fendus: tremblans, suans de crainte,
> Les hauts monts ont croullé: cette Majesté saincte

> Paroissant fit trembler les simples elements,
> Et du monde esbranla les stables fondements.
> Le tonnerre grondant frappa cent fois la nuë;
> Tout s'enfuit ...
>
> (ll. 140-146)

> Factique sunt sonitus, et fulgura, et tonitrua:
> et terraemotus factus est magnus ...
>
> (xvi. 18)

> Et omnis insula fugit, et montes non sunt inventi.
>
> (xvi. 20)

This description manifests the awe-inspiring power and majesty of God. But its resemblance to John's vision of final judgment at this early point in the poem imparts to it a significance as symbolic revelation. The presentation of God as "le bon Roy ... (qui) / Met l'espee au costé et marche à la vengeance" (ll. 137-38) and of physical upheaval referring specifically to the dissolution of aspects of terrestrial geography recorded in Revelation evokes the vengeance of God and the restoration of order which terminate the Apocalypse and thus anticipates the corresponding dénouement of *Les Tragiques*.

When the destruction of the wicked is accomplished at the end of history, the poet presents the new order of Heaven which awaits God's Elect as the celestial Jerusalem. He describes this wondrous city of Paradise in much the same terms as the apostle portrayed his vision of the reward of the just. The walls are studded with precious jewels and the city is illuminated by the glory of God's countenance. The grace of God satisfies the thirst of the Elect and the fruits of the Tree of Life provide their nourishment:

> ... Ô grand Dieu des armees,
> De ces beaux cieux nouveaux les voutes enflammees,
> Et la nouvelle terre, et la neufve cité,
> Jerusalem la saincte, annoncent ta bonté!
> ... Sion la bien-heureuse
> N'a pierre dans ses murs qui ne soit precieuse ...
> Nul de nous ne craint plus ni la soif ni la faim,
> Nous avons l'eau de grace et des Anges le pain; ...
> Plus ne faut de soleil, car la face de Dieu
> Est le soleil unique et l'astre de ce lieu.
>
> ("Jugement," ll. 1055-70)

> Et ego Johannes vidi sanctam urbem Hierusalem novam.
> (xxi. 2)
>
> Et fundamenta muri urbis omni lapide pretioso ornata.
> (xxi. 19)
>
> Neque urbs ista eget sole, vel luna, et luceant in
> ea: nam gloria Dei illustravit eam, et lucerna
> eius est Agnus.
> (xxi. 23)

The kingdom of Heaven is described in the poem as the "banquet où l'espoux nous invite" ("Jugement," l. 1155), and the "nopces de l'Agneau" ("Jugement," l. 1192). Both images evoke the marriage of the Lamb which characterizes the new order promised by the Book of Revelation: "Gaudeamus et exultemus, et demus gloriam ei: Quia venerunt nuptiae Agni et uxor eius paravit se" (xix. 7).

Les Tragiques is divided into seven books, and the number seven is the distinctive mark of the Apocalypse.[7] The apostle writes to the seven Churches of Asia; presents the opening of the seven seals by seven angels; describes the sounding of seven trumpets, the seven horns of the beast, and the seven bowls of the wrath of God. The parallel which has emerged between the images of the Book of Revelation and those of the poem allows the assumption that the seven books of *Les Tragiques* represent a conscious decision on the part of d'Aubigné to sustain and reinforce that parallel.

This correspondence of significant images extends the analogy between God's destruction of the beast (Pope) at final judgment in *Les Tragiques* and in Revelation on which Rocheblave based his impression that the poem represents a "Protestant Apocalypse."[8] But the Revelation of St. John is more than a compilation of distinct images; as a vision of the future directly inspired by Christ, it contains a message or lesson which God communicates to his servants by means of these symbols. In order for the parallel between the two works to be meaningful, a definite relationship must exist between the significance of d'Aubigné's symbols and that of the Biblical images. Moreover, the total lesson of both must be analogous

---

[7] Henri Bullinger, *Cent sermons sur l'Apocalypse de Jésus Christ* (1558), p. 12.

[8] Rocheblave, p. 83.

if the poem is truly to be considered an "apocalypse." The most natural and fruitful perspective on the comparison of *Les Tragiques* and the Book of Revelation will be provided by commentary representative of the sixteenth-century Protestant interpretation of St. John's prophecies. One such work is Henri Bullinger's *Cent sermons sur l'Apocalypse,* published in 1558. Bullinger, who was Zwingli's successor in Zurich, corresponded regularly with Calvin and was well known to Théodore de Bèze, who translated his *Perfectio Christianorum* into French in 1551. This association, and the fact that the sermons were published in Geneva by Jean Crespin, indicates that they can be considered a characteristic Huguenot explication of Revelation. Comparison of Bullinger's sermons with the *Paraphrase et exposition sur l'Apocalypse* of Pierre de Launay, published in Geneva in 1651, reveals no essential contradiction between the two works. This implies that the Protestant interpretation remains fundamentally unchanged during the ninety-three years which separate the commentaries. The thirty-nine years in which d'Aubigné wrote and revised *Les Tragiques* (1577-1616) fall within the period covered by Bullinger and Launay.

According to Bullinger, the Book of Revelation reveals God's ultimate justice at the end of history when the conflict between the forces of Good and Evil is resolved in final judgment. Satan, who is represented as a dragon, is God's opponent in this continuing struggle; he torments the just and is responsible for the deaths of the martyrs who remain true to God's word and faith. Satan's instrument of oppression in the Christian era has been the first beast, the Roman Empire, which through its emperors, the second beast, persecuted the early followers of Christ. From the Protestant point of view, these persecutions have continued to the present day, for as Rome became Christian, the Popes merely replaced their pagan predecessors; they have forsaken their spiritual responsibilities in a quest for temporal wealth and power. Thus the Apocalypse represents the papacy and the Pope as the fallen star, the two beasts, the whore — all symbols of the forces of Evil, and the enemies of God and His people. The juxtaposition of the Pope and the antichrist which was made almost instinctively by d'Aubigné ("Vengeances," l. 167) was just as natural for Bullinger: "Le pape donc est Antechrist, veu qu'il s'attribue ceste pleine puissance tant au ciel qu'en la terre ... Ceste beste furieuse est bien si audacieuse et outrecuidée de s'attribuer les deux cornes de l'Agneau: assavoir les deux puissances, Royale et Episcopale." [9] The papal persecution of "heretics" with whom the reformers felt an affinity, such as the Albigensians and Vaudois, proved to the Huguenot exegetes that the Catholic Church and its hierarchy were the heirs to the anti-Christian Roman emperors. [10] The Pope is Apóllyon and his clergy are the locusts which emerge from the pit of the abyss of Hell to torment the faithful. The center of this iniquitous activity is Rome, the successor to ancient Babylon; as Babylon persecuted God's chosen people, the Hebrews, and fostered idolatry, so its spiritual descendant murders the true Christian children of God, and worships the idols and images of the Apostolic Church.

If the Huguenot exegete sees the forces of Evil represented in the Book of Revelation as the Catholic Church, the forces of Good are those Christians who have opposed the religion of the Popes. The martyred souls under the altar are not only the first followers of Christ murdered by the emperors, or the early "heretics" martyrized by the Pope. They represent as well the Protestants against whom the papacy now wages a fierce campaign, for the images and lesson of the Apocalypse are applicable to all times in history. This conflict on earth is a manifestation of the continuing struggle between the angels of God and those of Satan. The discussion of the martyred souls, and of the persecuted Evangelical Church, evoked for Bullinger as it did for d'Aubigné the image of Abel ("Vengeances," ll. 155-160). The Biblical martyr is the archetype of the victims of the Roman Church and thus represents all those who have died for the true religion of God: "Abel a esté le premier martyr recueilli sous ceste autel: et apres luy ont esté recueillis tous ceux qui sont morts pour la religion." [11]

It is evident that the thematic content of the Book of Revelation as interpreted by Bullinger parallels the development of *Les Tragiques*. In both cases, a struggle is described between the same protagonists and antagonists; both works begin with the disordered situation of the continued success of God's enemies and the plea

---

[9] Bullinger, p. 54.
[10] Pierre de Launay, *Paraphrase et exposition sur l'Apocalypse* (1651), p. 416.
[11] Bullinger, pp. 230, 452, and 250.

of the martyred chosen people for vengeance. D'Aubigné believed that the time for the disappearance of the beast from the earth was near at hand, and that the number 666 represented the year 1666, when the world of Satan would come to an end. The century preceding this time is described in the poem as the world of tragic disorder (d'Aubigné's *monde à l'envers*). Bullinger himself, in commenting on the period before the thousand-year captivity of the beast, noticed the remarkable similarity between the description in Revelation and his own time:

> Et n'y aura que les malins qui soyent opulens et riches: mais les bons seront agitez par tous opprobres et outrages: et souffreteux. Toute droicture sera pervertie, toutes loix periront. Nul ne possedera rien alors qui ne soit mal acquis, ou iniquement defendu. La violence outrageuse et l'audace tiendront tout en subjection. Il n'y aura nulle fidelité ès hommes: il n'y aura nulle paix ny humanité, il n'y aura nulle honte ne verité. Y avait il description plus propre pour monstrer devant les yeux la condition presente de nostre temps? [12]

The beast's activity causes the same effects in the Apocalypse and in *Les Tragiques*. The pastor could have been commenting on the poem.

The poet and the apostle draw their knowledge from the same source. The poet reveals meaning in the world through a special relationship to God which allows him to view the human situation from a divine perspective. The origin of his insight as he progresses from scribe to prophet, to angel-like instrument of final justice, is always the Lord Himself. Similarly, the Book of Revelation is "Apocalypsis Jesus Christi quam dedit ipsi Deus": "Or l'autheur n'est autre que le Seigneur Dieu luy-mesme: voire le Dieu des saincts prophetes." Both works have been made possible because God deemed it important to open the gates of Heaven and make the essence of the divine order of the universe accessible to the faithful. D'Aubigné can say with Bullinger: "Et de fait le ciel nous est à present ouvert." [13]

---

[12] Bullinger, p. 767.
[13] Bullinger, pp. 864 and 246.

The most significant aspect of Revelation for the Huguenot exegete is the divine explanation of the meaning and purpose of the persecution of the faithful. Bullinger first remarks that God is aware of the affliction of His people; indeed, this torment is willed by the Divine and subsequently executed by Satan. Through suffering, the Lord tries the mettle and faith of His children, testing them as He did Job. The Protestant whose belief, like that of his Biblical counterpart, is strong enough to resist the devil's attempts to seduce him, is a monument to the greater glory of God. Moreover, death by fire purifies the souls of the martyrs, making them worthy of their reward of eternal life in Heaven:

> Il est bien vray, que le Seigneur Jesus donne puissance aux diables et aux hommes pervers sur ses serviteurs. Si cela vous semble estrange, oyons ce qui sensuit, afin que vous soyez esprouvez. Il n'abandonne point ses fideles à Satan, afin qu'ils perissent: mais à ceste fin qu'ils soyent esprouvez et examinez. Parquoy c'est à bonne fin que nous sommes mis au feu, à ce que nous soyons purgez de nos ordures et que la vertu de nostre foy reluise, et que Dieu soit glorifiez, et que nous soyons mieus purifiez.
>
> (Bullinger, p. 86)

Often the suffering of the faithful is brought about by their own perversity, but through God's grace this too becomes a test of faith (Bullinger, p. 622).

The paradoxical nature of martyrdom —torture, suffering, and death accompanied by joy and rebirth— is expressed in *Les Tragiques* by the image of "feux."[14] Fire for the martyr represents "les outils de sa mort, instruments de sa gloire / ... les armes de victoire" ("Feux," ll. 93-94). It cleanses his soul: "Les feux qui vous brusloyent vous ont rendus candides" ("Feux," l. 14), and it is the path to salvation, for the flames carry the soul to its eternal reward:

> ... le feu violent
> Ne brusloit pas encor son cœur en la bruslant;
> Il court par ses costés; en fin, leger, il vole
> Porter dedans le ciel et l'ame et la parole.
>
> ("Feux," ll. 203-206)

---

[14] See Chapter I, p. 21.

The faithful are led to the pyre of death where they die to be reborn into the new life. Thus they can say with understanding, "Heureux qui pour justice a l'honneur de souffrir" ("Feux," l. 84), for they know Christ's words, "quoniam illorum est regnum caelorum" (Matt. v. 10).

It is not a mere coincidence that the explanation of Protestant suffering which Bullinger finds in the text of Revelation is exactly that of d'Aubigné in *Les Tragiques*. The poem is based on the fundamental Protestant belief that events in the world are the result of God's providence. It is the intention of the poet to reveal this divine order of the universe to man incapable of understanding it alone. Bullinger reveals that the essence of the Book of Revelation is this concept of providence which God communicates to the faithful: "Car en ceste façon (through God's revelation) il nous monstre et enseigne de recognoistre la saincte et bonne providence de Dieu, sa bonne volonté envers nous, et son gouvernement tresjuste en toutes œuvres, et mesme au milieu des plus grieves calamitez et persecutions" (p. 177). From his limited perspective, man interprets the death of the Protestants as a defeat for God and His people. For those who understand the message of providence in Revelation, this martyrdom represents rebirth in the eternal afterlife of Heaven: "Que si la mort mesme ne nous estonne point outre mesure, mais si en la foulant aux pieds, nous nous offrons nous-mesmes à Dieu, voicy la promesse que Christ nous fait, qu'il nous donnera la couronne de vie" (Bullinger, p. 87).

> De qui veut vivre au ciel l'aise soit la souffrance
> Et le jour de la mort celui de la naissance.
>
> ("Feux," ll. 249-50)

Providence, as revealed by the poet and the apostle, justifies the affliction of the just and promises eternal salvation. The perverted success of the iniquitous is ordered through the vision of final judgment which guarantees the ultimate punishment of the wicked: "Il a fallu donc que ceste matiere des jugemens de Dieu ait esté amplement et diligemment traitée et mise comme devant les yeux des auditeurs, afin que tous entendissent quelle sera la fin indubitablement tant des meschans et infideles, que des bons et fideles" (Bullinger, p. 601).

D'Aubigné has, in effect, written a modern version of the Apocalypse. The images which define the content of the poem and that of the last book of the Bible are the same and their symbolic value is equivalent. The points of departure and subsequent thematic development of the two works are fundamentally parallel; the conclusions reached are analogous. Every interpretation which Bullinger makes of the Book of Revelation can be applied to *Les Tragiques,* and his sermons could be used just as meaningfully to explicate d'Aubigné's "Apocalypse."

Exegetes and commentators through the ages have interpreted God's intention in Revelation to be the consolation of the faithful. They see Him choosing to reveal the true meaning of terrestrial existence, at a time when the early Christians were being persecuted for the faith in Rome, in order to comfort His people. In times of adversity, Christian sects have traditionally turned to Revelation to renew their faith in providence and the promise of ultimate justice and salvation. Precisely because the lessons of Scripture are timeless, Bullinger addresses his congregation and, through the publication of his sermons, all his coreligionists, bringing them God's message of patience and faith at a time when they are maligned and persecuted (p. 88). Over and over again the pastor repeats the idea of consolation:

> Les fideles ont tousjours besoin de consolation spirituelle. Or ce livre ... en fournit abondamment.
> ("Preface")

> ... nous avons une bien grande consolation pour l'Eglise en ses adversitez, quand nous voyons que l'Agneau ouvre les sceaux, et que tout se fait par la providence de Dieu.
> (p. 33)

> L'Apostre continue à descrire la cité divine ou celeste, pour la consolation des fideles, et pour les conserver au milieu de toutes oppressions et tentations.
> (p. 845)

If consolation is the lesson of St. John's Book of Revelation, by analogy it is the lesson of d'Aubigné's "Apocalypse." The association of the two works implies that the poet meant to console and encourage his coreligionists, and to assure them of the reality of God's providence and ultimate justice:

Et certes selon la description de la tyrannie Romaine et de toute la faction de l'Antechrist, il pouvoit sembler que c'estoit fait de l'Eglise et de la prediction de l'Evangile, et que l'impieté triompheroit perpetuellement. Il expose donc par une fort belle vision, que Christ ne lairra pour cela de regner en ses fideles et eleus, qu'il sera victorieux, qu'il aura tousjours une Eglise... Il descrit quels doyvent estre les eleus de Dieu... Et davantage que Rome sera mise à bas, et tous les infideles seront punis... Et à celle fin que la consolation fust pleine et entiere, il adjouste que les fideles qui meurent en Christ, de la mort corporelle s'en vont droit obtenir la vie eternelle: ce qui peut grandement confermer et fortifier les esprits de tous les croyans, en quelque danger qu'ils se puissent trouver.

(Bullinger, p. 558)

Although written fifty-seven years before the publication of the poem, this commentary by Bullinger on chapter fourteen of Revelation is equally significant as a concise, though complete, statement of the purpose and theme of *Les Tragiques*. The two works are much closer chronologically than the 1616 publication date implies, for the poem belongs essentially to the major period of d'Aubigné's creative activity (1577-79), when conditions in France were more nearly similar to those of Bullinger's time (1558). Although the half-century which preceded Henri IV's accession to the throne marked the most troubled era of religious strife, the poem did appear when tension was mounting following the death of the king.[15] At a time when the Huguenots could anticipate a renewal of the Catholic campaign against them, d'Aubigné offered a message of hope and comfort to the faithful. The poem is truly the "Protestant Apocalypse," a contemporary restatement of Revelation.

II

The nature of *Les Tragiques* as a Protestant Apocalypse throws light on the question of "style" raised by the poet himself. Speaking as the artist removed from his work in "Aux Lecteurs," d'Aubigné

---

[15] Charles Bost, *Histoire des Protestants de France* (1957), p. 127.

specifically labels "Misères" *style bas et tragicque,* "Princes" and "Chambre Dorée" *style moyen,* "Feux" *style tragicque moyen* and "Fers," "Vengeances," and "Jugement" *style tragicque eslevé.* In the poem itself, as the poet in the act of creating, he speaks of *style inconnu* and *style sainct.*

The concept of poetic styles derives from the distinction in early Greek rhetoric between the pragmatic or plain style and the emotional or so-called grand style.[16] Cicero's definitions in the *de Oratore* (III, 177, 199, 212) and the *Orator* (99) of the three functions of oratory —*docere, conciliare, movere*— gave rise to a style which was the *tertium quid* between the plain and the grand. This tripartite division of style was formulated also in the *Rhetoric ad Herennium:*

> Sunt ... tria genera, quae genera nos figuras appellamus, in quibus omnis ratio non vitiosa consumitur: unam gravem, alteram mediocrem, tertiam extenuatam vocamus. Gravis est, quae constat ex verborum gravium magna et ornata constructione; mediocris est, quae constat ex humiliore, neque tamen ex infima pervulgatissima verborum dignitate; attenuata est, quae demissa est usque ad usitatissimam puri sermonis consuetudinam.
>
> (IV: 8)

The distinction between styles depends on the quantity and quality of the figures of elocution as well as the particular function of each.

Medieval rhetoricians assimilated the concept of three styles but redefined them to make subject matter —specifically the social status of the leading characters— rather than stylistic ornament the distinguishing factor. Jean de Garlande makes this distinction clearly in his *Poetria:*

---

[16] For a general discussion of the concept of style see G. L. Hendrickson, "The Origin and Meaning of the Ancient Characters of Style," *American Journal of Philology,* XXVI (1905), 249-90. Aristotle, in his discussion of style in the *Rhetoric* (III 2, 7), seems to be distinguishing between language as the objective medium for statement of fact or thought and language which also conveys the author's emotion or artistic feeling to his audience. Theophrastus advanced beyond his master in the explicit recognition of a style of language suitable to the pragmatic aspects of proof which was clearly separate from the artistic and emotional aspects of language.

> Item sunt tres styli secundum tres status hominim: pastorali vitae convenit stylus humilis, agricolis mediocris, gravibus personis quae praesunt pastoribus et agricolis. [17]

The so-called "wheel of Virgil," which indicated the social condition, proper names, and residences proper for the characters of each style, as well as the animals, instruments, and plants affiliated with them, provided the medieval writer with a graphic illustration of the connection between style and subject matter. Subject matter was still the determining factor of style in the 16th century. Pierre Fabri's *Le grand et vray art de pleine rhetorique* (1521) is an early example of a poetic which states this relationship; [18] Scaliger's *Poetices* is a later and more significant one.

The 16th-century poetics also considered subject matter to be the basis of generic distinctions. The traditional separation of comedy and tragedy, for example, was founded on the difference in the station of the characters each portrayed. Tragedy was considered one of the highest genres because it dealt with princes, kings, and important affairs of the state. Since the style of tragedy was necessarily high for the very same reasons, it is not surprising that genre and style became correlative notions. The Pléiade recognized the interdependence of genre, style and subject matter in Peletier's *Art poétique* where the style of tragedy, for example, which presents *grandes matières*, is characterized as sublime. [19] Both Scaliger, and more suggestive in a discussion of d'Aubigné, la Taille, made this association:

> La Tragedie donc est une espece et un genre de Poesie non vulgaire, mais autant elegant, beau et excellent qu'il est possible. Son vray subject ne traicte que de piteuses ruines de grands Seigneurs, que des inconstances de Fortune... [20]

Although Dr. Sauerwein recognizes style's connection to subject matter, and its subsequent relation to genre, he persists in equating

---

[17] Jean de Garlande, *Poetria* in *Romanische Forschungen*, Vol. XIII (1902), p. 920.
[18] W. Patterson, *Three Centuries of French Poetic Theory* (1935), p. 7.
[19] Peletier du Mans, *Art poétique*, ed. A. Boulanger (1930), p. 190.
[20] La Taille, *Art de la tragédie*, ed. F. West (1939), p. 24.

it with vocabulary, as regards d'Aubigné.[21] It is true that vocabulary is an aspect of style, for it communicates the subject matter in language suitable to it, but to equate the two is to ignore the contemporary literary context. Style, I propose, was understood most consistently in the 16th century in generic terms, and it is this perspective which allows us to appreciate d'Aubigné's apparently personal use of the expression *style tragicque*; Dr. Sauerwein's starting point leads him astray.

Because he denies the generic significance of the terms *tragique* and *tragédie* in the poem, Dr. Sauerwein does not consider style in terms of tragedy.[22] Instead, starting with what he considers to be d'Aubigné's use of the adjective *tragique*, he sees a suggestion of the "tragic style of a *hircinus cantus vel foetidus*," the medieval perversion of the Horatian concept of tragedy as goat song.[23] Since he defines style as vocabulary, he is led to characterize the vocabulary as "fetid" and to speak of the *style tragicque* as a *style puant*.[24] This *puant* or *fetide* style is, he claims, especially manifest in "Princes" and "Chambre Dorée" where it translates the "stinking" subject matter which relates to the Valois court, although he admits it as a common element in all seven books. The essential passage on which this view is based is found in "Chambre Dorée," and concludes on this note: "Fi des puants vocables." But by removing this line from its context, Sauerwein has rather seriously misinterpreted its meaning. At the end of the third book, having proceeded from a picture of the horrible truth about the princes, the poet moves to a celestial plane and describes the heavenly procession of Truth and Justice. Speaking of the *quatre licornes pures* (914) which represent virginity and purity, *la vefve et l'orphelin* (915), he then turns his attention to the judges. Suddenly, as if drawn irresistibly by a great magnet, this thought triggers the recitation of a long list of technical legal terms:

---

[21] Sauerwein, *op. cit.*, p. 110.

[22] In fairness to Dr. Sauerwein, he does attempt on one occasion to give *tragédie* a sliding meaning closer to my own: *ibid.*, pp. 119-120, but this is a momentary shifting of ground which confuses rather than clarifies.

[23] *Ibid.*, p. 108.

[24] *Ibid.*, pp. 107-111.

> Tout interlocutoire, arrest, appointement
> A plaider, à produire un gros enfantement
> De procez, d'intendits, de griefs ; un compulsoire,
> Puis le desrogatoire à un desrogatoire,
> Visa, pareatis, replicque, exceptions,
> Revisions, duplique, objects, salvations,
> Hypothecques, guever, deguerpir, prealables,
> Fin de non recevoir.
>
> (919-926)

It is against this jargon that he exclaims,

> ... Fi des puants vocables
> Qui m'ont changé mon style et mon sens à l'envers!
>
> (926-27)

The style, far from being *puant* in itself, is upset by the introduction of these "vocables." While speaking of heavenly things the poet was suddenly caught up in the basest of earthly things. The legal terms are spewed out as if to reject something horribly unpalatable; listed meaninglessly out of context, they ring false and hollow to evoke the perverted justice of the *monde à l'envers*. They are "stinking" and "noxious" when compared to the beauty and purity of true Justice, the unicorns, the widow and orphan who preceded. It is this divinely inspired vision, this style, which was distorted and debased by the thought of sordid injustice. It seems incongruous that the poet's use of *puant* in this instance should have been meant to apply as well to the content of the last book, "Jugement," with its vision of final judgment and of Heaven. Yet this is where Sauerwein's discussion must lead him once he defines *style tragicque* as *style puant*.

The historical considerations of style do shed light on the *style tragicque*. *Les Tragiques* contains a dramatic tragedy within the framework of an epic poem, and, traditionally, tragedy is written in a high and noble style to reflect the elevated rank and position of its major characters. Since, as Sauerwein himself does point out, d'Aubigné subscribed to the notion that style was based on content, it can be assumed that *style tragicque* is a high style reflecting the serious and elevated subject matter of the genre.[25] The protagonists,

---

[25] *Ibid.*, p. 103.

France and the true Christian Church, occupy exalted positions; the Protestant martyrs share this rank since they are characterized by the poet as kings in Heaven. The active roles of God and the poet as he becomes scribe, prophet, and instrument of final judgment, are essential aspects of that content. From a more technical, and a more medieval point of view, the poetic style is characterized by those ornaments which define the highest style. It contains metaphors, allegories, comparisons, hyperboles, prosopopeia, apostrophes, and antithesis; all figures which Peletier includes in his discussion of the ornaments of poetry (I, 9). It is also written in alexandrine verse, which he considered to be the most noble form of line. As a final consideration on this subject, let us note that the traditional function of the highest style from the time of Cicero was *movere*. [26] It is therefore wholly consistent that the poet's avowed purpose in *Les Tragiques* was *esmouvoir*. Henri Weber pays particular attention to this aspect of d'Aubigné's use of vocabulary and imagery in his chapter on the poem. [27]

Within the context of the *style tragicque* which applies to all seven books of the poem there is a progression of the subject matter from earth to Heaven. In this sense the content determines the evolution in style from *bas et tragicque* to *tragicque eslevé*. As Henry Sauerwein correctly indicates, the action of "Misères" takes place on earth; that of "Princes" and "Chambre Dorée" in Heaven as well as on earth, as the figure of God and the allegorical *filles de Dieu* are introduced; that of "Feux" in Heaven and on earth as the martyrs die and are assumed into Paradise; and finally that of "Fers," "Vengeances," and "Jugement" essentially in Heaven. [28] This movement from *bas* to *eslevé* also follows the increasingly celestial position of the poet. In the first book he sees the world about him from an entirely human point of view. In the books characterized as *moyens*, he is divinely inspired and shares God's vantage point. In the last three books, the poet moves closer to God as scribe, prophet, and instrument of final judgment.

The references to style which d'Aubigné makes within the poem as poet are more revealing than those made in the introduction as

---

[26] On style see Hendrickson, *op. cit.*
[27] Weber, *op. cit.*, pp. 677, 683.
[28] Sauerwein, *op. cit.*, pp. 108-121.

critic. The first reference appears in the "Préface en vers" where the poet speaks metaphorically of the subject matter and form of the poem as he sends it out into the world:

> Sois hardi, ne te cache point,
> Entre chez les Rois mal en point;
> Que la pauvreté de ta robbe
> Ne te face honte ni peur,
> Ne te diminuë ou desrobe
> La suffisance ni le cœur.
>
> Porte, comme au senat romain,
> L'advis et l'habit du vilain
> Qui vint du Danube sauvage,
> Et monstra hideux, effronté,
> De la façon non du langage,
> La mal-plaisante verité.
>
> (13-24)

The *vilain ... du Danube* is an anecdote in the *Libro del Emperador Marco Aurelio con relox de principes,* of Antonio de Guevara, published in Spain in 1529, and translated into French in 1531 and 1555. It relates the story of an old German rustic who revealed to the Roman senate the iniquitous rule of its governors in the provinces. While his appearance shocked the sophisticated senators, the truth and wisdom of his words earned their respect. He was frightful and offensive in dress and manner, in the form of his message, and audacious by his presence in that august assembly and by the nature of the subject he proposed. But the substance of the words he spoke, the counsel he offered, was truth.

The poet personifies his poem to make it analogous to the rustic. The paucity of its exterior covering, or form, is suggested through images of dress: *la pauvreté de ta robbe* and *mal en point*, poorly clothed. The parallel extends as well to the matter they present, for the essence of the poet's words is truth. The reference to the form as *mal en point* is due, perhaps, to the poet's humility, but it is more likely that it results from his desire to de-emphasize the significance of the form to concentrate the reader's focus on the soul of the poem, the content of truth. The modesty of the exterior, he implies, allows the interior to stand out:

> Ta trenche n'a or ne couleur,
> Ta couverture sans valeur
> Permet, s'il y a quelque joye,
> Aux bons la trouver au dedans;
> Aux autres fascheux je t'envoye
> Pour leur faire grincer les dents.
>
> ("Préface," 31-36)

Like the peasant, the poem exposes the iniquitous rulers and promises their inevitable punishment. To be forced to recognize themselves and their actions will be a terrible experience, as d'Aubigné's images indicate.

The truth which the poem represents is, as we have seen, God's revelation to the poet. A reference in the "Préface" expresses this divine dimension in terms of a Biblical metaphor:

> Je commençois à arracher
> Des cailloux polis d'un rocher,
> Et elle (truth) tordoit une fonde;
> Puis nous jettions par l'univers,
> En forme d'une pierre ronde,
> Ses belles plaintes et mes vers.
>
> (157-62)

As David chose the stones and slew Goliath with his slingshot, so the poet and truth will propel their stone, which is the poem, and slay the modern giant. The poet, like David, battles in the name of God: "Ego vero venio ad te in nomine Jehovae exercituum" (I Sam. 17:45). A final element is added to the association between the poet, his poem, truth and God as Truth leads the poet to the Church. As the poet envisions the Church's struggle to accomplish her destiny in the face of the wicked designs of her adversaries, or as he describes this conflict through his poetry, his sight and his soul are ravished to Heaven:

> Je sens ravir dedans les cieux
> Mon ame aussi bien que mes yeux,
> Quand en ces montagnes j'advise
> Ces grands coups de la verité,
> Et les beaux combats de l'Eglise.
>
> (187-91)

Here is an image of the Church at war, with Truth as its weapon, and a divinely inspired poet who views and records the struggle.

The situation resembles the picture already presented of the poet, inspired by a *sainct amour* and armed with Truth, who is going to do battle for the Church. *Les Tragiques* is a war: "Puisqu'il faut s'attaquer aux legions de Rome, / Aux monstres d'Italie ..." ("Misères," 1-2), and the poem itself represents "Ces grands coups de la verité / Et les beaux combats de l'Eglise."

The references to the poet's state of divine inspiration or possession suggest the Platonic notion of divine furor, which became an important element in the aesthetic thought of the Renaissance with the introduction of Ficino in France. Sebillet affirmed in his *Art poétique françoys* (1548) that poetry is divinely inspired:

> Car le Poete de vraye merque, ne chante ses vers et carmes autrement que excité de la vigueur de son esprit, et inspiré de quelque divine afflation. [29]

Le solitaire premier (1552) of Pontus de Thyard interprets poetic furor as the *ravissement* and awakening of the soul to knowledge and truth, the first step in the elevation which leads it back to God. Ronsard insisted on the divine vocation of the poet, who, under the inspiration of the muses, reveals knowledge and truth to men:

> Le jour que je fu né, Apollon qui preside
> Aux Muses, me servit en ce monde de guide,
> M'anima d'un esprit subtil et vigoureux,
> Et me fit de science et d'honneur amoureux,
> En bien des grands thresors et des richesses vaines
> Qui aveuglent les yeux des personnes humaines
> Me donna pour partage une fureur d'esprit
> Et l'art de bien coucher ma verve par escrit. [30]

Montaigne too, experienced the poetic sally:

> Je la sentois naistre, croistre et augmenter en despit de ma resistance, et enfin, tout voyant et vivant, me saisir et posseder, de façon que comme d'une yvresse, l'image des

---

[29] Quoted from Weber, *op. cit.*, p. 109.
[30] Ronsard's "Elégie à Jacques Grévin," quoted from Patterson, *op. cit.*, p. 514.

> choses me commenceoit à paraistre aultre que de coustume.[31]

Montaigne resists the sally precisely because it is *erreur*, a straying from the human, the natural. Yet he fully appreciates the insights he gains and seems almost to regret its passing. Unlike d'Aubigné, for whom the furor is truly *saincte,* Montaigne's sally is not due to divine intervention and is characterized by his ambivalent attitude of awe and rejection.

The poet first mentions style in the poem itself when he declares that he now dares to bare the filth of the Valois court as the subject of "Princes": "Subject, stylle inconnu: combien de fois fermee / Ai-je à la verité la lumiere allumee?" (21-22). Without giving a precise indication of what is meant by style—except by relating it closely to content—the poet clearly reveals that he intends to combat evil by exposing it to the light of truth. With God's encouragement (42), he invokes Truth in terms which recall the Biblical metaphor of the "Préface":

> Preste-moi, verité, ta pastorale fonde,
> Que j'enfonce dedans la pierre la plus ronde
> Que je pourrai choisir, et que ce caillou rond
> Du vice-Goliath s'enchasse dans le front.
>
> (45-48)

Here again, when the poet speaks of subject matter, he implies that his poem is truth, divinely inspired to fulfill the will of God.

Now that he is writing *Les Tragiques,* the poet turns his back on the love poets who, like himself up to the present, "ne chantent... / Que miel, que ris, que jeux, amours et passe-temps" (65-67). "Ce siecle," he declares, "autre en ses moeurs, demande un autre style" (77). The harsh realities of the contemporary world have made love poetry inappropriate, frivolous and even insensitive. The "Thessaly" of the past, with its lovely valleys ("Misères," 69) and silver streams ("Misères," 59), where the idle poets drew their inspiration ("Misères," 60), has been sullied and brutally threatened by the wicked who seek to destroy her. A tragedy is now being played out

---

[31] Montaigne, *Les Essais,* ed. Villey (1922), II, 12, "Apologie de Raymond Sebond."

on the stage of France ("Princes," 80-84); history requires that poetry abandon the delights of love and the pleasant life for the useful ("Princes," 72). Art, the poet infers, must be an instrument of truth, committed to the elucidation of political, social and ultimately, religious reality.

The substance of "Princes," verses 59-100, supports the view that style means vocabulary which accurately reflects the subject matter. The poet defends his heated expression (59) and the massacre, horror and bloodshed he portrays ("les vocables d'art de ce que j'entreprens" 64) in these terms. These same lines, by linking style to the qualities of *doux* and *utile,* suggest that it is more than vocabulary for it distinguishes between different types of poetry. Style is the basic poetic structure which characterizes *Les Tragiques.* Subject matter is Truth of fact; style is Truth of expression and form in relation to that fact. The fact, expression and form of *Les Tragiques* are based on the truth of God's revelation which the poem presents as divine tragedy and in its function as a new book of the Bible, the Protestant Apocalypse. It is especially revealing that the poet introduces the actual dramatic tragedy at this point to show how he has responded to the exigencies of the time:

> La main peut s'endormir, non l'ame reposer,
> Et voir en mesme temps nostre mere hardie
> Sur ses costez jouër si dure tragedie,
> Proche à sa catastrophe, où tant d'actes passez
> Me font frapper des mains et dire: c'est assez!
>
> (80-84)

The significance of what d'Aubigné called the *style sainct* ("Jugement," 362) now emerges clearly. It is, as Sauerwein indicated, the divine inspiration of the poet as he moves closer to his God through the last books of the poem.[32] It includes, as well, the countless scriptural elements—images, expressions, phrases, names and grammatical constructions—which infuse the text with Biblical authenticity.[33] The general characteristics which Henri Weber identifies as taken from Scripture are also part of the *style sainct*: the

---

[32] Sauerwein, *op. cit.,* pp. 173-212.
[33] J. Trénel has identified 664 such instances in his *L'Elément biblique dans l'œuvre poétique d'Agrippa d'Aubigné.*

history of the Hebrews; that of the early Christians and the corruption of Rome which form the Biblical background to the modern situation; the Psalms and prophetic speeches which are adapted to the contemporary world; the visions of God in Heaven; the antithetical structure of the Bible which contrasts the ordeal of terrestrial existence with the peace and fulfillment of the celestial afterlife.[34] In "Vengeances" the poet explicitly encourages the impression that one is reading Scripture. The Bible represents God's word and if read in the light of grace can reveal His truth; so it is with the poet's book, the words he is presenting: "Ainsi les visions qui seront ici peintes / Seront exemples vrais de nos histoires sainctes" (89-90).

The *style sainct* is thus more than the theme of an inspired poet and the presence of certain Biblical elements. It is divine truth revealed to the modern prophet which assumes the form and expression of the Book of Revelation. The new Apocalypse contains scores of images and expressions drawn from other books of the Old and New Testaments just as its original counterpart does. The grammatical constructions imitated from the Hebrew recreate the vocabulary and syntax of Scripture.[35] The beasts, dragons, devils and whores depict a contemporary world which recalls that exposed by the prophet of Patmos. The rugged, unadorned style of Scripture which for Calvin was a sign of Biblical truth is the style of *Les Tragiques*.[36] The antithesis between life on earth and the afterlife in Heaven, whose resolution defines the very structure of the poem, is the paradox at the center of John's Revelation. Within the world of art the poet as prophet has revealed God's Truth in what now stands as a new book of the Bible. This is the *style inconnu*; this is the *style sainct*.

---

[34] Weber, *op. cit.*, pp. 607, 705.
[35] Trénel, *op. cit.*, pp. 93-103.
[36] Jean Calvin, *Institution de la religion chrestienne*, I, viii, 1.

Chapter IV

ART AND THE INSPIRED POET

Les Tragiques abounds in historical fact. Real events and personages build up the *monde à l'envers* of "Misères" to expose the national and religious tragedy; their presence is required as well for the satire of "Princes" and "Chambre Dorée." The force of the poem as a modern Apocalypse depends on the re-creation and interpretation of the contemporary scene. Small wonder, then, that critics have considered *Les Tragiques* as an historical panorama of the times, a guide to innumerable military encounters, public events, kings, princes and martyrs.

The difficulty which arises from this view is indicated by the reaction of Garnier and Plattard to the portrait of Richard de Gastines in "Feux." In a long and eloquent speech (ll. 739-958), Gastines consoles and encourages his coreligionists with a depth of compassion and wisdom far beyond his actual years. The editors attempt to reconcile the apparent incongruity between historical fact and poetic presentation:

> Richard, contemporain d'Agrippa, devait avoir environ dix-huit ans quand il montra cet admirable courage devant la mort. Mais les circonstances et les responsabilités avaient déjà pu le mûrir précocement, car il était marié et père de famille et cela rend un peu moins extraordinaire "la grande doctrine," l'expérience et la philosophie de la vie que lui prête le poète.
>
> (Note to "Feux," l. 974)

In a poem in which the action takes place on a stage encompassing heaven and earth, in which angels, devils, and allegorical figures abound, d'Aubigné's primary concern is not verisimilitude in any narrow sense. The poet's role as scribe and prophet, the dream or mystical vision which inspired the poem, the precise description of a given historical figure or battle are all open to the charge of historical inaccuracy or distortion. What Garnier, Plattard and others fail to appreciate is that *Les Tragiques* is not intended as a mimetic re-presentation of contemporary people, places and events. As art it is the product of an inventive imagination which absorbs and transmutes history's raw material into the ordered, structured and meaningful world of the poem. D'Aubigné's subject is present-day history; his purpose is to uncover its significance; his means is poetry. Through the metaphorical structure of tragedy and apocalypse, the apparently senseless turbulence of historical events gives way to purpose and design, and a pattern of ordered movement. D'Aubigné enjoys an aesthetic and spiritual perspective from which contemporary phenomena gain a meaning indiscernible to one caught up in the swell of events. He records and interprets the sense of the world about him, functioning at that point at which history merges with art.

I

D'Aubigné exists outside the poetic world of *Les Tragiques*. The topos of the stolen manuscript, which opens the prefatory "Aux lecteurs," distances him from the work to focus attention on the poem and its poet within: it underscores *Les Tragiques* as fiction and warns against a simple historical or biographical reading. D'Aubigné is responsible for the structure of the poem and for the levels of imagery, metaphor and thematic development by which it emerges as tragedy and apocalypse. Within the poetic world, the narrator is a poet who is writing the work; he is a character in the action, functioning as narrator-poet, actor, scribe, prophet and historian.

The episode of the *tableaux célestes* in "Fers" clearly distinguishes d'Aubigné from the poet of *Les Tragiques*. These paintings, which place current battles within the context of providential design, are a fiction created by d'Aubigné to give meaning to contemporary events. For the narrator-poet, privileged by divine inspiration to stand with the elect in Heaven, these canvases are the handiwork of the angels, executed upon their return from the terrestrial battlefields. He moves among them, recording what he sees, transmitting the true reality there portrayed. The poet is as much a product of d'Aubigné's inspired imagination as the *tableaux* themselves.

Within the context of *Les Tragiques* the narrator-poet functions as the fictional analogue of d'Aubigné: he strives to render contemporary reality meaningful. Often he acts merely as an observer, as when he beholds the *tableaux*, transmitting divine meaning as it is revealed to him. At other times, his art becomes the active means through which value and significance emerge. In "Feux," he consecrates a martyrology *pour example,* to teach his coreligionists the lesson of faith and courage. Out of the apparently senseless slaughter of thousands of innocent Protestants, the poet chooses and arranges individual martyrs ("Je veux tirer à part la constante Marie" l. 529) in an order and structure which gives each event a value. The presentation brings to life figures who no longer exist in the world of men:

> Je ne t'oublieray pas, ô ame bien heureuse!
> Je tireray ton nom de la nuict tenebreuse;
> Ton martyre secret, ton exemple caché
> Sera par mes escrits des ombres arraché.
> (ll. 993-96)

The poet recalls the martyred child and she is resurrected through the poem (*relever* suggests both recall and rebirth) to live again in men's hearts and minds: "Du berceau, du tombeau je releve une fille" (l. 997). The juxtaposition of "berceau" and "tombeau" implies that as the cradle was the child's tomb, so the tomb cradled her as she was reborn to the spiritual afterlife. The Protestant martyr, the poet assures us, enjoys new life in God's eternal Heaven.

In "Vengeances," the poet structures and arranges events to disclose three eras in which divine retribution has been wrought: Old Testament, early Christian, contemporary Protestant. From this chronology, which allows the circumstances of the past to shed light on those of today, the true movement of history emerges. We see the poet at work as he makes his way through the countless instances of God's vengeance—the poetic raw material—including or excluding individual examples for poetic reasons: "Mais le trop long discours de ces notables morts / Me fait laisser à part ces vengeances des corps / Pour m'envoler plus haut..." (ll. 931-33). If he loses his reader in tedious detail or description, or if he fails to make the transition from one subject to another at the proper moment, truth will be obscured and will fall victim to the mediocrity of his art. The success of the poem as history depends on its quality as a work of art.

The poet's effort to disclose the true meaning of history through his poem reflects the artistic activity of the angels who execute the *tableaux célestes* described in "Fers" (ll. 261-). Upon their return from the terrestrial battlefields, the angels depict the armed conflict consuming the Protestants and Catholics in France:

> Chacun des esprits saincts ayant fourni sa tasche
> Et retourné au ciel comme à prendre relasche,
> Representoit au vif d'un compas mesuré,
> Dans le large parvis du haut ciel azuré,
> Aux yeux de l'Eternel, d'une science exquise,
> Les hontes de Satan, les combats de l'Eglise.
>
> (ll. 267-72)

These paintings do not reproduce the chaos and confusion which envelop contemporary events and cloud their significance. With sublime knowledge and skill ("d'une science exquise"), the angels give to reality an order ("d'un compas mesuré") which reveals meaning. As the last line of the quotation infers, and as the rest of "Fers" confirms, the canvases communicate the true sense of the battles by disclosing their place in God's providential design. Each representation depicts another step in the progression of the chosen people and its church, through trial and tribulation, to final judgment and eternal salvation in Heaven.

Under the paintings the angels add a gloss which translates the significance of their artwork into prose:

> Dieu met en cette main la plume pour escrire
> Où un jour il mettra le glaive de son ire :
> Les conseils plus secrets, les heures et les jours,
> Les actes et le temps sont par songneux discours
> Adjoutés au pinceau ; jamais à la memoire
> Ne fut si doctement sacré une autre histoire,
> Car le temps s'y distingue, et tout l'ordre des faits
> Est si parfaitement par les Anges parfaits

> Escrit, deduit, compté, que par les mains sçavantes
> Les plus vieilles saisons encor y sont presentes.
>
> (ll. 307-316)

Granted divine insight to expose secret machinations and to uncover hidden motives, they record the events and describe the personages of history. From the turmoil and anarchy of human activity, an essential pattern and order is disclosed ("tout l'ordre des faits"). These artists are Heaven's historians: they picture the true dialectic of historical progression, portray the vital force which animates that movement, and represent the temporal and spatial importance of the events which mark its path. Here, in the celestial realm, in the juxtaposition of the paintings and the prose gloss, the true history of the world is recorded: "Dans le ciel, desguisé historien des terres, / Ils (the Elect) lisent en leur paix les efforts de nos guerres" (ll. 323-24).

The poem is divine history. It differs only in its scope and in its verse from the *pesante histoire* the poet proposes to write some day to celebrate the Protestant cause ("Feux," ll. 37-52). It fulfills the function which d'Aubigné poses as the purpose of history in the preface to his *Histoire universelle*: "le vrai fruit de toute l'histoire... est de connoistre en la folie et la faiblesse des hommes le jugement et la force de Dieu."[1] The narrator-poet, through his art, discloses the working out of God's providential design.

II

The many roles which the narrator plays as poet, prophet and historian are hard to keep separate and distinct and often they appear to merge and overlap. He describes what takes place in Heaven as an outside observer ("Misères," ll. 450-60; "Chambre Dorée," ll. 1-190; "Feux," ll. 1-18, 1083-93; "Fers," ll. 1-108); reads and records God's innermost thoughts and reactions ("Misères," l. 683; "Princes," l. 391; "Feux," l. 613; "Fers," ll. 1-18); reproduces the *tableaux* which he sees in Heaven ("Fers"); acts as an instrument of celestial vengeance on earth ("Jugement," ll. 7-8),

---

[1] Agrippa d'Aubigné, *Histoire universelle*, ed. A. de Ruble (1886), p. 10.

and speaks as a poet about writing the poem ("Feux," ll. 19-52, 527-29, 713; "Fers," l. 1191). The narrator will interrupt a description and break a dramatic effect which has been building up to address his readers directly ("Misères," l. 1073; "Princes," l. 399; "Chambre Dorée," l. 595; "Feux," l. 1093; "Fers," l. 1025). In "Feux," what begins as the presentation of a painting depicting past events in their true historical perspective seems to come to life with God's appearance (ll. 147-   ). The *tableau* becomes the original drama as it unfolds before God's and the narrator's eyes. All through "Feux" there appears to be a confusion between events as they originally took place and as they are recreated in the *tableaux célestes*.

These shifting roles and sliding planes of reality are effects of the divine inspiration which the narrator enjoys as poet and prophet. In "Fers" (ll. 1195-1206) he describes the experience which has enlightened him and compelled him to write the poem. His soul was ravished, he tells us, and carried to the ethereal realm where it beheld "les beaux secrets et tableaux que j'escris" (l. 1200). The narrator purposely hedges between stating catagorically that he has experienced a true vision and admitting that it was a dream: "Soit qu'un songe au matin m'ait donné ces images, / Soit qu'en la pamoison l'esprit fit ces voyages. / Ne t'enquiers, mon lecteur, comment il vid et fit" (ll. 1201-1203). The reader remains uncertain whether he is dealing with a human phenomenon, created out of the fertile imagination of a devoted Huguenot or with a divine presence. This ambiguity recalls our earlier discussion of the poet's use of *quelquefois* in the context of inspiration in the "Préface." [2] Although the poem, in general, is written under God's guidance, we suggested that only *quelquefois* does the poet's soul attain the heavenly heights. The point at which dream or poetic invention merges into vision is not distinct. Within the world of *Les Tragiques* there is no constant vantage point; rather, there is a moving perspective which ranges back and forth between the terrestrial and celestial realms. We stand, in a sense, between two worlds, where time and eternity overlap, where space and infinity coexist, experiencing the transition of the terrestrial universe as it evolves into the Kingdom of Heaven.

---

[2] See p. 48.

The time structure of *Les Tragiques* reflects the juxtaposition of the two realms in which the poet operates. As a man, he shares the fear and consternation of his coreligionists when he confronts the contemporary scene. His religion has taught him that the march of history traces a linear progression, according to God's preordained plan, from Eden to Christ to Judgment Day, from the creation and fall of man through his redemption to eternal salvation or damnation. But the lessons of faith are often difficult to sustain. In the midst of upheaval, persecution and chaos, the divine chronology is obscured: the past and its lessons are forgotten, the present is misunderstood or ignored, the future appears unknown and unknowable. Instead of recognizing the succession of the three chosen peoples—Hebrews, early Christians, Protestants—each a degree nearer to God, the Huguenot imagines a cyclical pattern which repeats the downfall of each elected people and thus predicts the destruction of his own church. Confined by nature to a present from which he cannot distance himself, inherently weak and perverse, owing even his desire for good to the gift of grace, his faith wanes and his religious conviction ebbs.

When the poet shares God's vantage point, the whole universe comes into focus. From Heaven, time does not exist as past, present and future. All of human history from the creation to the end of the world appears an eternal present: "Dieu vid en mesme temps (car le prompt changement / De cent ans, de cent lieux ne luy est qu'un moment) / Deux rares cruautez..." ("Feux," ll. 147-49). God's providential design is made manifest as events and individuals reveal their essential relationship to one another and to the overall context of that design. The poet is depicted ranging over all of history (unconcerned by spatial or temporal confines), choosing martyrs at will, juxtaposing Biblical, early Christian and modern history, recording the secrets of future events. The destinies of the three chosen peoples merge through analogy to assume a single significance which transcends time and space. The present recalls the past which illuminates and informs it, and points in turn to the future to which it imparts meaning. Past events, which in the world are fixed and set, exist in a eternal present as a living reality. Future happenings, vague and ephemeral as we predict or imagine them, come vividly to life as they will occur. Temporarily freed from the restrictions of chronological time, the inspired narrator views history as an eternal panorama unfolding before his very eyes.

The tension between the narrator as a man and as a divinely inspired poet and prophet is maintained through *Les Tragiques*. The terrestrial and celestial perspectives are juxtaposed until the culmination of "Jugement" when they fuse into eternal timelessness. Certain developments in the introductory half of that last book prepare for the final apotheosis by introducing elements of the real into the visionary until description wholly becomes reality. Here we can plot the movement by which the terrestrial universe is absorbed by the Kingdom of Heaven. Final judgment, depicted as future, has already begun.

The poet's knowledge of divine reward or punishment which he is about to disclose as God's agent indicates the reality of the vision: "Qui seront les premiers sur lesquels je desploye / Ce pacquet à malheurs ou de parfaicte joye" (ll. 21-22). This divulgence will cause initial pleasure or pain in the manifestation of ultimate justice. The joy or suffering which is the essence of the eternal afterlife proceeds from this point in the poem.

The close resemblance of contemporary events to the description of the end of history represents a second indication of the reality of the future. The vision of forthcoming judgment foretells of the brutality, rape, murder, hunger and suffering Paris will endure as the beginning of eternal punishment for her crimes: "Or cependant, voici que promet seurement, / Comme petits portraits du futur jugement, / L'Eternel aux meschans" (ll. 217-19). These circumstances, however, have already occurred with the siege of the capital in 1590. The war, plague and famine which raged at the time recall God wreaking vengeance in the Bible. The modern prophet's threat to Paris ("Il attache à ton dos la devorante peste, / Et le glaive et la faim..." ll. 268-69) echoes Jeremiah's warning to the iniquitous Hebrews: "Quoniam gladio et fame et peste consumam" (XIV: 12). It conjures up as well the four riders of the Apocalypse (VI: 1-5), symbols of the devastation and destruction of the old order which precedes the end of time.

The address to the perfidious apostates again overlaps the present situation and what is to come. The cowardly, vicious betrayal of God and the true Church reveals that final judgment is at hand:

> Quand le terme est escheu des divines justices,
> Les cœurs abastardis sont infectés de vices;
> Dieu frappe le dedans, oste premierement
> Et retire le don de leur entendement ...
> Il fait fondre le cœur et secher le courage.
>
> (ll. 211-16)

The poet declares in verse 663 that time has reached the end promised by the prophets, that the kingdom of God has arrived: "C'est fait, Dieu vient regner; de toute prophetie / Se void la periode à ce poinct accomplie" (ll. 663-664). With his eyes turned toward the *chemin des cieux,* he describes the resurrection of the flesh as if it were all happening there before him. The use of the present tense reinforces this impression:

> La terre ouvre son sein, du ventre des tombeaux
> Naissent des enterrés les visages nouveaux;
> Du pré, du bois, du champ, presque de toutes places
> Sortent les corps nouveaux et les nouvelles faces.
>
> (ll. 665-68)

> Les cendres des bruslés volent de toutes parts;
> Les brins plustost unis qu'ils ne furent espars
> Viennent à leur posteau, en cette heureuse place,
> Rians au ciel riant d'une agreable audace.
>
> (ll. 681-84)

Then, turning to the *saincts escrits,* the poet portrays a vision which appears to be stimulated by the reading of Scripture. Again, the scene takes place before his very eyes: "Des-jà l'air retentit et la trompette sonne, / Le bon prend asseurance et le meschant s'estonne" (ll. 699-700). The intensity of these visions and the continuing use of the present tense succeed in giving them actual existence for the reader.

Before the condemnation of the iniquitous, the poet addresses a prayer for guidance to the Holy Spirit:

> Condui, trés sainct Esprit, en cet endroict ma bouche,
> Que par la passion plus exprés je ne touche
> Que ne permet ta regle, et que, juge leger,
> Je n'attire sur moi jugement pour juger.
>
> (ll. 803-806)

He begins with the Pope whom he judges and damns to eternal perdition as "antechrist" and "Apollyon" (ll. 811-854). The poet portrays the *aisné fils de Satan* and his wicked accomplices standing before the *gueule de l'enfer* which opens impatiently, awaiting the signal to engulf them forever. Standing beside the divine throne he records God's promise of salvation to the just: "Vos pechés sont esteints, le Juge est vostre frere; / Venez donc, bien-heureux, triompher pour jamais / Au royaume eternel de victoire et de paix" (ll. 876-878). At these words, the universe changes miraculously into the new order, undergoing a metamorphosis of eternal beauty symbolic of the rebirth of the righteous souls:

> A ce mot tout se change en beautés eternelles.
> Ce changement de tout est si doux aux fidelles!
> Que de parfaicts plaisirs! O Dieu, qu'ils trouvent beau
> Cette terre nouvelle et ce grand ciel nouveau!
>
> (ll. 879-82)

God then condemns the wicked forever (ll. 887-92) and the poet depicts with frightening immediacy the cataclysmic upheaval of the universe which accompanies their descent into Hell. He addresses the damned souls directly as he conjures up the terror of the endless torment which awaits them:

> Les Satans decouplés d'ongles et dents tranchantes,
> Sans mort, deschireront leurs proyes renaissantes;
> Ces demons tourmentans hurleront tourmentés, ...
> Ils vengeront sur vous ce qu'ils endureront.
>
> (ll. 1035-42)

The most terrible punishment the wicked must endure is an awareness of the eternal Heaven. Here, the poet turns his gaze upward to attempt to express the ineffable beauty of the celestial afterlife. He records the hymn of the seraphim which describes the new Jerusalem and then breaks his description to anticipate his readers' questions as they try to understand Heaven in their own terms: "On s'enquiert si le frere y connoistra le frere" (l. 1107); "Ainsi dedans la vie immortelle et seconde / Nous aurons bien les sens que nous eusmes au monde" (ll. 1199-1200). Intermittant vision and imaginative projection into the future finally merge at the end of the canto: "Chetif, je ne puis plus approcher de mon œil / L'œil du ciel; je ne puis supporter le soleil" (ll. 1209-10).

The content of the last part of "Jugement" recalls the end of history in St. John's Book of Revelation. Yet there is a fundamental difference between the two works which is pointedly manifested by the verb tenses in each. The visions which God discloses to the apostle, and which are related in the Apocalypse, all refer to a future time in history. Since John transcribes what he saw into the words of his Book after this revelation takes place, he uses the past tense almost exclusively: "Tum vidi bestiam e mari ascendem ..." (13:1); "Qui apprehendit draconem ... et vinxit eum ad annas mille" (20:2); "Tum quintus angelus clanxit, et vidi stellam e caelo cecidisse in terram, et data est ei angelo clavis putei abyssi" (9:1). The present tense is used in direct quotations: "Et dixit mihi, Fuerunt, ego sum A et Ω" (21:6), and when the apostle turns to speak directly to his readers to introduce a vision or comment on it: "Hic tolerantia sanctorum est; hic qui observant praecepta Dei, et fidem Jesu" (14:12); "Haec est resurrectio prima. Beatus et sanctus qui habet partem in resurrectione prime" (20:5,6). The future tense describes what is to come: "Et audivi vocam magnam ... Ecce tabernaculum Dei est cum dominibus et habitabit cum eis" (21:3).

Unlike the apostle, the poet is not recounting a vision which has already taken place, but one which is happening before his very eyes; hence the predominant use of the present tense at the end of the poem. The past tense is used only to recall the iniquity of the wicked and to describe the conditions in which the apostles have lived in Heaven (ll. 1159-80). The poet's use of the future, however, appears to conflict with the immediacy of these visions, for it indicates that final judgment has not completely evolved. The poet's concern, his way of seeing things when he addresses the iniquitous and his audience directly is an essentially human one; his visions of the end of time are divine. The tension between the intense accumulation of present visions and the intermittant projection into the future is resolved as the two merge in a present reality:

> Chetif, je ne puis plus approcher de mon œil
> L'œil du ciel; je ne puis supporter le soleil.
> Encor tout esbloüi, en raisons je me fonde
> Pour de mon ame voir la grand' ame du monde,

> Sçavoir ce qu'on ne sçait et qu'on ne peut sçavoir,
> Ce que n'a ouï l'oreille et que l'œil n'a peu voir;
> Mes sens n'ont plus de sens, l'esprit de moy s'envole,
> Le cœur ravi se taist, ma bouche est sans parole:
> Tout meurt, l'ame s'enfuit, et reprenant son lieu
> Exstatique se pasme au giron de son Dieu.
>
> (II. 1209-18)

The poet has moved as close to God as an angel, or the apostle John, but he has remained essentially human, his soul still lodged in his body. The verb *se fondre* indicates a physical melting which frees the spirit and allows it to know what is not known and cannot be known by mortals. It represents as well the fusion of present and future in an eternal present which is the Kingdom of Heaven. As *tout meurt*, the soul takes its place on high and swoons ecstatically in the bosom of its God. The poet has been assumed into immortality, as he said the living would be, at the time of final judgment.

III

As divine inspiration opens up the celestial realm to the narrator-poet, he faces the imposing task of communicating what he is privileged to see and understand to his earthbound readers. How can he convey knowledge which lies beyond the ken of ordinary mortals? How can he impart the secrets of Heaven with a language rooted in human experience? The narrator, as poet and prophet, attempts to render the divine accessible through the use of metaphor and symbol. He represents personages, places and concepts unknown to his readers by evoking images familiar to them. The poetic richness of the language at his command allows the celestial and its significance to emerge by suggestion, implication and inference.

While the national disorder in France is presented for the most part as direct description, it relies heavily on metaphor for its expressive force. Historical reality, difficult to grasp in its totality, is depicted as tragedy; the players and the action assume tangible, visible and common shapes. France, and the abstract concept of nation, become a mother, a giant, a ship, each presentation complementing the others, each communicating the sense of impending disaster in an identifiable, even personal way. The treachery of the princes turns them into snakes; their lasciviousness into birds. The poet pictures virtuous nobles as mountains and the columns and dome of God's temple. All through "Misères," "Princes" and "Chambre Dorée" truth is disclosed metaphorically: the bankers are stomachs poisoning the body of France; Catherine is a hydra, a beast, a sorceress, a snake; the royal court an avernus; the judges cannibals and wolves. The allegories of Fortune and Virtue in "Princes" and of the court of Injustice in "Chambre Dorée" operate in a similar way to concretize abstractions and make them forceful and present. Justice and piety, avarice and hypocrisy are not theoretical concepts; they are vital notions which are sustained or destroyed by human attitudes. And whether they live or not affects men in a very real way, as the situation in contemporary France demonstrates.

When the narrator sets about to present God, his task becomes all the more formidable for to describe the ineffable is a contradiction in terms. As he opens the scene of the Lord in Heaven in "Fers," he faces the problem directly and indicates its solution:

> Ainsi (sans definir de l'Eternel la place,
> Mais comme il est permis aux tesmoignages saincts
> Comprendre le celeste aux termes des humains)
> Ce gran Roy de tous rois, ce Prince de tous princes,
> Lassé de visiter ses rebelles provinces,
> Se rassit en son throsne et d'honneur couronné
> Fit au peuple du ciel voir son chef rayonné.
>
> (ll. 18-24)

Les Tragiques is a new book of the Bible, a *tesmoignage sainct* which represents God and His word to man in terms he can understand. The inspired narrator, as the author of the work, transposes what he sees into the human idiom, in an attempt to make his words convey at least the feeling of divinity.[3] The universe is

---

[3] Sauerwein points out, in his *Agrippa d'Aubigné's Les Tragiques,* p. 82, n. 29, that d'Aubigné relies heavily on images of light to describe objects and realities not known to humans. He suggests that d'Aubigné can only visualize Heaven in these terms. While this is in part true, the poet, when inspired, does experience Heaven directly. The problem seems rather to communicate this experience to "mere" mortals. Light is a human image which conveys a sense of God.

pictured as a great kingdom over which God rules as king. All mortals —princes and paupers alike— as his subjects owe Him fealty, love and respect, and He in turn looks after them as a father for his children, a shepherd for his flock. He weeps over the torment of the good and wrathfully punishes the wicked. All through the poem the anthropomorphic presentation of God dominates to allow the reader to experience the divine essence.

Symbol and parable function similarly to uncover the working of providence. The poem, as Protestant Apocalypse, draws a vocabulary from Revelation which strikingly expresses the contemporary situation. By picturing the Catholic Church as a whore and her priests as *puantes chenilles*, the poet translates both the abominations they commit and the danger they represent; by portraying the precarious existence of the Protestant Church as a pregnant woman forced to flee into the desert to escape her oppressors, he fixes its desperate and vulnerable position. Abstract moral values become concrete and recognizable through their association with colors. Black is used as the symbol for evil and is linked with the Catholics and their crimes; red, as the color of spilled blood and the fires of persecution represents their iniquity; white evokes the purity of the Huguenots.[4] In his symbolic use of colors, as in his use of the imagery of Revelation, d'Aubigné consciously drew on a long and established Biblical and literary tradition. He was aware that this vocabulary carried with it certain connotations and associations which could enrich and broaden the poetic context of *Les Tragiques*. Our discussion of word clusters and of the analogy with the Book of Revelation has touched on this subject. At the same time, d'Aubigné appears to have appreciated the expressive force of this language. The striking visual and tactile quality of his imagery, and its emotive effect, allow the reader to feel the poet's inspired experience. The degree to which the divine reality becomes concrete and real determines the degree to which the poet realizes his goal of *esmouvoir*.

Parables such as the presentation of Ocean which concludes "Fers" (ll. 1447-1532) communicate the sense of history. The poet

---

[4] See Sauerwein who discusses the symbolism of colors all through his study of *Les Tragiques*, and H. Weber, *La création poétique en France au XVIe siècle* (1956), pp. 687-705.

describes a vision in which a Neptune-like figure, awakening from a long sleep, unwittingly rejects the bodies of God's martyred children. After the angels descend to gather their spilled blood, Ocean perceives his error and lovingly embraces the broken and tortured bodies to preserve them until their resurrection at final judgment. The parable discloses the eventual reward of the just and guarantees salvation for the unburied thousands whose deaths, unnoticed and unmarked by men, have been recorded by God for all time. Here, as in the Bible, metaphor allows man to "comprendre le celeste aux termes des humains."

IV

The narrator-poet uses a vocabulary of light to transcribe the ineffable majesty of God and the beauty of Heaven and to set them off from the darkness and obscurity of Satan and his followers.[5] At the same time, the related image pattern of sight-blindness serves metaphorically to distinguish the righteous from the iniquitous, those who receive God from those who reject Him.[6] Within the context of *Les Tragiques* as the last book of the Bible, these images echo the language of the Gospel, recalling the miracles of blind men cured by Christ to see and believe and His own use of the metaphor in John (chap. 9:39): "Et dixit Jeschua, Ad judicium mundi huius veni, ut ii qui non vident, videant: et qui vident caeci fiant."

Sight in the framework of *Les Tragiques* means above all the faculty to recognize and acknowledge truth through belief in the one

---

[5] This vocabulary, drawn from established Biblical and literary tradition, makes use especially of words like *soleil, lumière, flambeau, reluire, briller, clair, flamboyant*. Sauerwein examines the cluster *lumière-obscurité* as part of the dramatic alignment of the poem (pp. 82-83). Weber identifies images of light which evoke God in his glory (pp. 694-97).

[6] Even critics who have recognized the significance of light imagery in *Les Tragiques* overlook the function of sight-blindness. In reviewing the allegorical vices in "Chambre Dorée," Sauerwein says, "There is no apparent scheme in the treatment of parts of the body, even though the most consistently used is the eye" (p. 86). In a footnote he adds, "As a conscious artist d'Aubigné may be using the eye within the poetry to reinforce both his own and the reader's ability to 'see' the abstract vices. In terms of cultural tradition outside the poetry, the function of the eye in Augustinus as the seat of concupiscence may also have found its place in this book."

true God. Those who realize that they stand in the dark before the Lord are illuminated by the divine radiance and granted the power of heavenly vision. In its light they distinguish a new order —providential design— and the values deriving from divinity which shape the Protestant religion as a way of life. This spiritual insight, symbolized by the narrator's vantage point in Heaven, can also bring terrestrial events into focus. In the world of *Les Tragiques,* the responsibility for seeing clearly and understanding is placed squarely on the individual. No longer does God speak directly and personally to His people —as in the time of the Old and New Testaments— or work prodigious miracles which compel men to believe. Today, the narrator tells us, truth itself is present in a divinely enlightened world and it must be sought and acknowledged: "Nous vivons en clarté, / Et à l'œil possedons le corps de verité" ("Vengeances," ll. 755-56). With the inner eye, the soul, which the narrator calls *des yeux du ciel* ("Feux," l. 857), man must strive to see clearly, for true sight precedes true life: "Je viens à vous ... / Et à qui m'entendra, comme Paul Ananie, / Ambassadeur portant et la veuë et la vie" ("Jugement," ll. 23-26). As the author of a new Revelation, the narrator-poet-prophet, privy to the secrets of Heaven, provides the spiritual lens through which truth can be perceived and eternal life achieved.

The chosen possess a clear and shining eye, indicative of their belief in God and symbolic of their exalted status ("Chambre Dorée," l. 825; "Feux," l. 168). Meek and humble, aware that through grace and faith alone they derive all good from God, the faithful make no pretense of knowing and they enjoy true vision:

> Blanche fille du ciel (Truth), flambeau d'Eternité!
> Nul bon œil ne la void qui transi ne se pasme,
> Dans cette pasmoison s'esleve au ciel tout ame;
> L'enthusiasme apprend à mieux cognoistre et voir.
>
> ("Princes," ll. 176-79)

The martyr, who bears witness to his commitment to God by words and by actions (etymologically the word martyr comes from the Greek where it means a witness), keeps his eye fixed on Heaven: "Œil qui fiché au ciel ... / Ne jette un seul regard pour eslongner sa veuë/Du seul bien" ("Feux," ll. 169-171). He perceives God with new eyes ("Feux," l. 211) and dies so that others might see and believe ("Feux," ll. 223, 385, 695, 981). The poet depicts the martyr at the stake as a beacon radiating divine truth ("Mais bruslant il faloit luire à la verité. / L'homme est un cher flambeau ... "Feux," ll. 368-69) which lights the way to salvation: "O bienheureux celuy qui, quand l'homme le tue, / Arrache de l'erreur tant d'esprits par sa veuë" ("Feux," ll. 981-82). To those who see in the spiritual sense, the martyr's death is a rebirth into the kingdom of Heaven and thus an act worthy of imitation. The poet recalls instances where the witness to martyrdom himself becomes a martyr to bear witness ("Feux," ll. 251-54).

The wicked, in their arrogance, claim to see and to know all when in fact they remain blind to God and to truth ("Vengeances," l. 259): ...vos foibles veuës / Ne sceurent onc passer la region des nuës (ll. 505-506).[7] Their field of vision has been confined to the terrestrial realm and even here they have had myopic sight. The iniquitous have been led astray, dazzled by the false luster of worldly ends ("Princes," ll. 1338-40). Enchanted as if under a diabolic spell, their gaze remains fixed; they do not see the crimes committed all around them and they are even blind to the reality of their own evil ("le peuple n'a des yeux à son mal" "Fers," l. 989). Although the wicked witness martyrdom, they act as unmoved spectators, and when they imitate, it is the erroneous and evil practices of the unenlightened pagans ("Feux," l. 1327). The poet's plea for divine vengeance would make their punishment fit the crime: "Que ceux qui ont fermé les yeux à nos miseres / ... Trouvent tes yeux fermez à juger leurs miseres" ("Misères," ll. 1357-61).

The symbol of spiritual blindness is the imperfect or ugly eye which distorts beauty, truth and goodness. The narrator-poet stresses the deformed and deforming eye in his presentation of the allegorical vices of "Chambre Dorée": Envy's eyes are *creux*, Hypocrisy's are *chassieux*, Inconstancy's *louches*, Vanity's *incertains*, Treason's *esgarés* and Cruelty's *de travers, flambans, veineux*, and *tremblans*. When Satan appears before God in "Fers," disguised as his former self, his eyes are described as "clairs et beaux, / Leur

---

[7] The context does not reveal whether they refused to see God, or could not because God had previously blinded them. Their ambiguous position between innocence and responsibility discussed earlier is thus underlined. See pp. 36-37, 52-54.

fureur adoucie" (ll. 43-44). As the omniscient God picks him out of the heavenly host ("aussi tost l'œil divin / De tant d'esprits benins tria l'esprit malin" 39-40), the apparent angel metamorphoses back into the devil. His eyes, as the mirrors of his soul, become "yeux flambants dessous les sourcils refroncés" (l. 56), or as it was more forcefully expressed in an earlier manuscript, "ses deux yeux en la teste horribles, enfoncez." All through *Les Tragiques,* the eye serves to indicate the fallen state of the damned. Catherine de Medici possesses a "basilique veuë" ("Misères," 1.894) which kills whatever it gazes upon. The perverse princes have "lousches veuës" ("Princes," l. 609), sly and defiling leers. The archetype of the wicked is Esau, who lives again in contemporary France as Charles IX, "de qui le ris, les yeux / Sentoyent bien un tyran" (ll. 765-66).

The vocabulary of vision operates prominently within the context of the dramatic tragedy. The narrator, at first an uninterested spectator, moves into the action to turn the eye of truth ("Princes," l. 451) on the wicked and their iniquity. Inspired by the prophets of old, he acknowledges his responsibility: "Là où estoyent les feux des prophetes plus vieux, / Je tends comme je puis le cordeau de mes yeux" ("Misères," ll. 27-29). As we saw earlier, the protagonists of both the national and religious tragedies—France, the Protestant Church and the wicked Catholics alike—have become blind to the righteous way and to the consequent disaster they court. The inspired poet's effort to resolve the tragedy is presented as his elevation to Heaven where he beholds divine truth and communicates it to his coreligionists. Their task, on the other hand, is to view and understand the word pictures he paints in order to learn God's oft-concealed meaning:

> Œil, qui as leu ces traits, si tu escoute, oreille,
> Encor un peu d'haleine à sçavoir la merveille
> De ceux que Dieu tira des ombres du tombeau.
> Nous changeons de propos. Voy encor ce tableau
> De Bourge: ...
>
> ("Fers," ll. 1121-25)

The spiritual rebirth of the just at the end of time is described metaphorically in terms of light and sight. Heaven ravishes human eyes to allow man to see in the Kingdom of Heaven:

> Une autre volonté et un autre sçavoir
> Leur arrache des yeux le plaisir de se voir,
> Le ciel ravit leurs yeux : des yeux premiers l'usage
> N'eust peu du nouveau ciel porter le beau visage.
>
> ("Jugement," ll. 705-708)

The clouds which have veiled God's presence part to reveal all the heavens as a single radiance. When the poet reaches the end of his appointed mission, his own assumption into Heaven is expressed with this imagery. His earthly eyes can no longer endure the brilliance of divinity. The poet's physical self gives way, as if melting under the sun's intense heat, freeing his soul to gaze directly upon God:

> Chetif, je ne puis plus approcher de mon œil
> L'œil du ciel ; je ne puis supporter le soleil.
> Encor tout esbloui, en raisons je me fonde
> Pour de mon ame voir la grand' ame du monde.
>
> (ll. 1209-1212)

CONCLUSION

The literary activity of the second half of the sixteenth century in France flourished in a world in which strong temptations of disintegration were setting in. To the spiritual disorder caused by the Reformation, the cataclysmic civil wars added shocks to the moral, social and political fabric of society. The uncertainty created by the existence of two Churches, two truths, two Antichrists was heightened by the brutal excesses of internal strife which led d'Aubigné to portray a *monde à l'envers*. The folly of man's endeavors, the frailty of his principles and the vulnerability of his aspirations were continually exposed. *

The frivolous preoccupation of the Valois court with masks and masquerades during this period of steadily worsening conditions reflects the sense of instability which dominated the contemporary view of man and his world. This phenomenon was not by any means limited to the sixteenth century; the seventeenth century, despite the picture often presented of order and harmony, was also characterized by games and the ballet, and the same is true of the eighteenth-century roccoco. But the mask was introduced into France from Italy during the Renaissance at a time when the world was in flux. Brantôme reports Henri II and his courtiers riding through the streets of Paris, masked and in costume, "rivalisant entre eux à qui faisait plus de follies." [1] D'Aubigné acridly pictures Charles IX and Henri III parading in the city dressed as women and depicts

---

* For an interesting discussion of this aspect of the Renaissance in France see H. Weber, *La création poétique au XVIe siècle en France* (1956), pp. 1-106.

[1] H. Prunières, *Le ballet de cour en France avant Benserade et Lully* (1913), pp. 37-38.

their ladies pursuing illicit amorous adventure under the cover of disguise. Within this historical context, we may say that by donning a mask, the wearer could change his being; an infinite number of masks meant an infinite number of personalities. A simple play of the imagination transformed Henri II into a carefree cavalier and made Henri III a lady of the court. The world of flux and movement recognized each as legitimate for it possessed no absolute against which to judge; truth was relative to the individual's perspective.

In this climate in which the aspiration to truth, knowledge, order and permanence became increasingly difficult to realize as the century progressed, art offered an instrument for coping with reality. Spectacle allowed elusion and escape; by fusing the masquerade and the joust, ballet, myth and pomp, it juxtaposed and intermingled the real and the imaginary to create a fabulous world of magic and fantasy.[2] Literature provided a means to confront reality metaphorically through satire or to replace it by a universe of order and harmony—that of the scientific poet, the lover, the visionary—controlled by the poet as its creator. Although the monumental dimensions of *Les Tragiques* as tragedy and Apocalypse, history and art clearly set it apart from the main literary currents of the time, it stands with much of contemporary literature as a reaction to the historical condition, an expression of the artist's aspiration to order.

The appearance of scientific poetry during the years 1562-1587 stems from the association of poetry and the Platonic notion of divine furor. Sebillet, Thyard, Ronsard believed that the poet, schooled in a vast general culture and knowledgeable in science, could be possessed by a furor which allowed him to penetrate the hidden significance of nature and the universe, and to understand cosmic relationships. Behind apparent confusion and contradiction, he perceived meaning and structure which he recorded and communicated as his art. Even without reference to poetic furor, the enlightened poet acquired a special status. Thyard's Curieux, exalting science as the means to knowledge, pictures the relationship of the man of learning to his world in these terms: "mercy des sciences, le sage est estimé demeurer au monde, come en une republique de laquelle il est chef, où il n'y a rien dont la disposition ne soit

---

[2] For a discussion of spectacle in the second half of the 16th century see Prunières, *Ibid*.

escrite et portraite en son esprit, tellement qu'il comprend en soy tout ceste univers, c'est à dire, la disposition bien ordonnée de tout." [3] From still another point of view, scientific poetry can be seen as an attempt to deal with a chaotic and apparently senseless reality by compiling all that was known about science and the universe in order to build up a coherent vision of the world. [4]

The lyric poetry which dominates the period, the bucolic idylls, eclogues, chansons and love poems, diverted the mind from the apocalyptic upheaval, as d'Aubigné himself suggested ("Princes," ll. 65-68). The popular and highly developed practice of love poetry, which owed its vogue in great measure to the prestige enjoyed by Petrarch and the Italian neo-Petrarchan poets, allowed escape into a world in which the lover is motivated by the single obsessive desire for the physical or spiritual possession of his lady. Using the traditional sonnet form—itself an ordered structure which fixes fleeting thoughts and emotions—and stylized language, themes and images to present a conventionalized love dialectic, the poet created a reality of permanence, order and stability. [5] The more chaotic the existential situation became, the more he appears to have abandoned the personal mode of expression to conform to literary and social custom. The use of Petrarchan themes became more abstract, less individual, and the sonnet sestet, long an object of experimentation, hardened into two set forms. [6] Ronsard stands virtually alone in resisting this tide. Drawing on his vast erudition and from the physical nature he loved, he combined the personal and innovative with the traditional. By manipulating and varying the form, he evoked the mutability of the life he loved and the destructive nature of time and death; by maintaining the conventional pattern he conserved the framework within which to pose his utopian dream.

---

[3] Pontus de Thyard, "Le premier curieux" in *The Universe of Pontus de Tyard*, ed. J. Lapp (1960), pp. 4-5. The discourse appeared in 1557, 1578 and 1587.

[4] Odette de Mourgues, *Metaphysical, Baroque and Précieux Poetry* (1953), pp. 31, 38.

[5] W. Monch, "Le sonnet et le platonisme," *Congrès de Tours et de Poitiers*, Association Guillaume Budé (1954).

[6] For the development of Petrarchan themes see G. Weise, "Manierismo e Letteratura," *Rivista di letteratura moderne e comparate*, XIII (1960), 5-52; for the sonnet form see M. Jasinski, *Histoire du sonnet en France* (1903), p. 105.

After Ronsard's essentially fruitless search for truth and knowledge which the *Hymnes* represent, it is significant that he returned to the love sonnet, for here, at least, he could find order and stability.

Ronsard's ambivalent longing to possess this reality in flux and permanence as well reflects the paradox which animates the poetry of Jean de Sponde. Like his predecessor, Sponde's desire to overcome inconstancy and the inexorable movement of time found expression in the love sonnet, where the stability of his devotion stood against the transitory nature of reality. But the poet disavowed the secular preoccupation of his youth which paled before the permanence which religion promised: "Beaux sejours, loin de l'œil, pres de l'entendement, / Aux prix de qui ce temps ne monte qu'un moment, / Au prix de qui le jour est un ombrage sombre, / Vous estes mon desir." [7] This spiritual aspiration, however, did not release Sponde from an irresistible attraction to the world, its beauties and delights. Torn between spirit and flesh, the poet of the *Stances* and *Sonnets sur la mort* expresses the tension and anxiety of the paradox he lives. Whereas art and religion offered d'Aubigné a means of coping with reality, Sponde never succeeded in sustaining his aspiration either in life or in art.

This brief glimpse of the climate of the times provides a basis for relating *Les Tragiques* to the literature of its period. A comparison of the poem with Montaigne's essays, for example, points up the role art plays in the quest for truth and order which underlies each work. D'Aubigné sought to transcend the physical and spiritual torment inflicted on the true Christian to pose a vision of peace and stability. He used satire to break down contemporary reality symbolically, and divine tragedy and apocalypse to replace it with the kingdom of Heaven. The poet's subject is the ultimate meaning of history, past, present and future; literature functions as a lens which brings providential order and design into focus.

The *Essais* also reflect a turbulent, chaotic and uncertain reality but the perspective is individual and personal rather than cosmic, secular rather than religious. Montaigne's search for order and stability found expression in his essays through which he came to know and accept himself and the human condition. These trials

---

[7] *Sonnets sur la mort*, VI, in A. M. Schmidt, *Les poètes du XVIe siècle* (1953), p. 896.

of his judgment, as he ranged from one subject to another, taught him that happiness could be realized by putting himself in harmony with the world of time and death, vicissitude and change. By riding with flux, he could find order and meaning in movement.

Another basis for relating *Les Tragiques* to contemporary literature has been provided by recent studies in the baroque which have identified striking aspects of style, content and spirit recurring in works of the period: metamorphosis, movement, paradox, spectacle, physicality.[8] The *monde à l'envers* which d'Aubigné presents appears to be a prototype of the baroque world: unstable, illusory, inverted, without fixed points of reference. The sliding perspective as the narrator ranges between earth and Heaven reflects motion and change. The language of the poem is violent, dynamic, concrete; its imagery, plastic, suited to transpose the abstract into physical terms. There is an emphasis on detail—the horrors of war, persecution, death—on the colors red and black and on the vocabulary of light, all elements of style which critics have identified as baroque.[9]

The usefulness of this approach to artistic unity has been diluted, however, by the tendency to define baroque by the mere presence of these characteristics.[10] Little attempt has been made to determine the function given elements fulfill within a particular work in that fusion of matter and form which makes great art unique. D'Aubigné's *monde à l'envers* is a world without God, a reality which appears to be an end in itself. The poet's intent through *Les Tragiques* is to establish a higher perspective which integrates this world into the order and pattern of divine providence, where every action, every thought is purposeful and meaningful. As we read the poem, we experience movement, flux and sliding vantage points but as a part of a "becoming" which is evolving inexorably toward "being." Once the celestial realm has been opened to the inspired poet, terrestrial disorder is progressively assumed into divine order. In other terms, the divine tragedy is resolved. The

---

[8] See I. Buffum, *Agrippa d'Aubigné's Les Tragiques* (1951); J. Zeldin, "*Les Tragiques* and the Baroque," *L'Esprit Créateur*, Vol. I, no. ii (1961), 67-74.

[9] See Buffum, *Ibid*.

[10] See H. Sauerwein's *Agrippa d'Aubigné's Les Tragiques* (1953), pp. 13-21 for a critique of Buffum; also Weber, *Ibid.*, pp. 686-87.

narrator's changing perspective does expose the antithesis between earth and Heaven, between disorder and order, but it does not express the personal tension between spirituality and physicality reminiscent of the works of Sponde, or of Donne; nor is the paradox left unresolved. Once the absolute focus is posited early in the work, the final outcome is never in doubt, even when the narrator's inspirational force wanes and he is left to cope with reality on his own. Change, flux, motion are revealed to be elements of a greater harmony or design—out of discord, there emerges concord.[11] D'Aubigné poses the "baroque" world to replace it with a spiritual vision; his model is St. John's Book of Revelation.

Similar remarks can be made about the style of *Les Tragiques*. The stress on the physical is not gratuitous, nor an end in itself, but rather recalls the focus of the Old Testament prophets. The poet's emphasis on death mirrors contemporary concerns and accentuates the traditional theme of death as spiritual rebirth. He is not obsessed with the image of light; he uses it, as Dante before him, to express the beauty and majesty of divinity which, after all, lies at the heart of his work.

In all, *Les Tragiques* appears more closely related to the Bible and to a general western-European literary tradition than to a vague notion of late 16th-century baroque which attempts to point up the unity of contemporary literature and to link it with the plastic arts. In the search for unity, due stress must be placed on individuality. Out of the heart and mind of the Huguenot poet, steeped in Biblical tradition, imbued with religious conviction, confident of his salvation and secure in his mission, *Les Tragiques* was created as divine tragedy and Protestant apocalypse to comfort and encourage the faithful at a time of impending disaster. The genius of d'Aubigné is that with elements often familiar—be they called Biblical or baroque—he fashioned a work unique in the history of western literature.

---

[11] For the notion of *concordia discors* see L. Spitzer, *Classical and Christian Ideas of World Harmony; Prolegomena to an Interpretation of the Word "Stimmung"* (1963), p. 9.

SELECTED BIBLIOGRAPHY

I. Works cited in the text

Aubigné, Agrippa d'. *Les Tragiques*. Eds. A. Garnier et J. Plattard. Paris, 1932. 4 vols.

——. *Œuvres complètes*. Eds. Réaume et Cassade. Paris, 1863-1892. 6 vols.

Bost, Charles. *Histoire des protestants de France*. Carrières-sous-Poissy, 1957.

Buffum, I. *Agrippa d'Aubigné's Les Tragiques*. New Haven, 1951.

Bullinger, Henri. *Cent sermons sur l'Apocalypse de Jesus Christ*. Geneva, 1558.

Calvin, Jean. *Institution de la religion chrestienne*. Ed. Abel Lefranc. Paris, 1911. 2 vols.

Calvin, Jean. *Joannis Calvini opera quae supersunt omnia*. Eds. G. Baum, E. Cunitz, E. Reuss. Brunsvigae, 1892. 59 vols.

Cicero. *De Re Publica*. Loeb Classical Library. Cambridge, 1943.

Doumergue, Emile. *Jean Calvin, les hommes et les choses de son temps*. Lausanne, 1899-1927. 7 vols.

Else, G. *Aristotle's Poetics: The Argument*. Cambridge, 1957.

Garlande, Jean de. *Poetria*. Romanische Forschungen (XIII), 1902.

Garnier, A. *Agrippa d'Aubigné et le parti protestant*. Paris, 1928. 3 vols.

Gmelin, H. "D'Aubigné als Dichter französischen Schicksals," Neuphilologische Monatsschrift, VIII (1937), 33-56.

Hendrickson, G. L. "The Origin and Meaning of the Ancient Characters of Style." American Journal of Philology, XXVI (1902), 249-90.

Huguet, E. *Dictionnaire de la langue française du seizième siecle*. Paris, 1925- .

Jasinski, Max. *Histoire du sonnet en France*. Paris, 1903.

Kern, Edith. *The Influence of Heinsius and Vossius on French Dramatic Theory*. Baltimore, 1949.

Lancaster, H. C. *The French Tragi-Comedy*. Baltimore, 1907.

Lanson, G. "L'idée de la tragédie en France avant Jodelle," RHL, XI (1904), 541-585.

LAUNAY, PIERRE DE. *Paraphrase et exposition sur l'Apocalypse, tirée des sainctes Ecritures et de l'histoire.* Geneva, 1651.
LA TAILLE, JEAN DE. *De l'art de la tragedie.* Ed. F. West, Manchester, 1939.

MONCH, W. "Le sonnet et le platonisme," Congrès de Tours et Poitiers, Association Guillaume Budé. Paris, 1954.
MONTAIGNE. *Les Essais.* Ed. Pierre Villey. Paris, 1922.
MOURGUES, ODETTE DE. *Metaphysical, Baroque and Précieux Poetry.* Oxford, 1953.

PATTERSON, W. F. *Three Centuries of French Poetic Theory.* Ann Arbor, 1935.
PELETIER DU MANS, J. *L'art poétique.* Ed. A. Boulanger, Paris, 1930.
PLATTARD, J. *Une figure de premier plan dans nos lettres de la renaissance, Agrippa d'Aubigné.* Paris, 1931.
PRUNIÈRES, H. *Le ballet de cour en France avant Benserade et Lully.* Paris, 1913.

RAYMOND, M. *L'influence de Ronsard sur la poésie française.* Paris, 1927.
ROCHEBLAVE, S. *Agrippa d'Aubigné.* Paris, 1910. 2 vols.
RONSARD, PIERRE DE. *Œuvres complètes.* Ed. G. Cohen. Paris, 1958.

SAINTE-BEUVE. *Tableau historique et critique de la poésie française et du théâtre français au XVIe siècle.* Paris, 1869.
SAUERWEIN, H. *Agrippa d'Aubigné's Les Tragiques.* Baltimore, 1953.
SEBILLET, TH. *Art poetique.* Ed. F. Gaiffe. Paris, 1910.
SPINGARN, J. *Literary Criticism in the Renaissance.* New York, 1899.
SPITZER, L. *Classical and Christian Ideas of World Harmony; Prolegomena to an interpretation of the word "Stimmung,"* Baltimore, 1963.

THYARD, PONTUS DE. "Le premier curieux," *The Universe of Pontus de Thyard.* Ed. J. Lapp. Ithaca, 1960.
TRENEL, J. *L'élément biblique dans l'œuvre poétique d'Agrippa d'Aubigné.* Paris, 1904.

WALKER, J. A. "D'Aubigné's Les Tragiques: A Genre Study." UTQ, XXXIII (1964), 109-124.
WEBER, H. *La création poétique au XVIe siècle en France.* Paris, 1956.
WEINBERG B. *Critical Prefaces of the French Renaissance.* Evanston, Ill. 1950.
WEISE, G. "Manierismo e letteratura," Rivista di letteratura moderne, XIII (1960), 5-52.

ZELDIN, J. "Les Tragiques and the Baroque," L'esprit créateur, I, no. 2, 67-74.

II. *Works helpful to the preparation of the text*

BALMAS, E. "Aubigné, poeta barocco." Le Lingue Straniere, 9,4 (1960).
BENSIMON, M. "Essai sur Agrippa d'Aubigné." SFr, VII (1963), 418-37.
BUSSON, H. *Les sources et le développement du rationalisme dans la littérature française de la renaissance.* Paris, 1922.

CHARBONNIER, A. *La poésie française et les guerres de religion.* Paris, 1919.

FARAL, E. *Les arts poétiques du XIIe et du XIIIe siècle.* Paris, 1924.

FLICHE, A. and MARTIN, V. *Histoire de l'église depuis les origines jusqu'à nos jours.* Paris, 1936- . 21 vols.

GRAY, F. "Variations on a Renaissance theme: The Poetic Landscape and a stance of Agrippa d'Aubigné." Philological Quarterly, XLIV (1965), 433-44.

GRIFFEN, R. "The Rebirth Motif in Agrippa d'Aubigné's Le Printemps." FS, XIX (1965), 227-38.

JONKER, G. *Le protestantisme et le théâtre de langue française au XVIe siècle.* Groningen, 1939.

KEEGSTRA, P. *Abraham sacrifiant de Théodore de Bèze et le théâtre calviniste de 1550-1566.* The Hague, 1928.

KRISTELLER, P. O. *Studies in Renaissance Thought and Letters.* Rome, 1956.

LANSON, G. "Etudes sur les origines de la tragédie classique en France." RHL, X (1903), 177-231, 413-36.

LEBEGUE, R. *La tragédie religieuse en France.* Paris, 1924.

LOUKOVITCH, K. *L'évolution de la tragédie religieuse classique en France.* Geneva, 1933.

MOORE, W. G. *La réforme allemande et la littérature française.* Strasbourg, 1930.

NOTHNAGLE, J. *Imagery in the Poetry of Agrippa d'Aubigné.* (Unpublished dissertation, University of Wisconsin, 1959).

RAYMOND, M. *Baroque et renaissance poétique.* Paris, 1955.

RAYMOND, M. "Le baroque littéraire français." SFr, XIII (1961), 23-39.

ROUSSELOT, JEAN. *Agrippa d'Aubigné.* Paris, 1966.

ROUSSET, J. *La littérature de l'âge baroque en France.* Paris, 1953.

ROUSSET, J. "Les images de la nuit et de la lumière chez quelques poètes religieux." CAIEF, no. 10 (1958), 58-68.

SCALIGER, J. C. *Poetices Libri Septem.* Lyons, 1581.

SONNENFELD, A. "The Development of an Image in the Work of d'Aubigné." Rom. Notes, II, i (1960), 42-44.

WEINBERG, B. "Scaliger versus Aristotle." Modern Philology, XXXIX (1942), 337-60.

WELLECK, R. "The Concept of the Baroque in Literary Scholarship." Journal of Æsthetics and art, V (1946), 77-109.

YOURCENAR, M. "Agrippa d'Aubigné," NRF, IX (1960), 819-34.

The Department of Romance Studies Digital Arts and Collaboration Lab at the University of North Carolina at Chapel Hill is proud to support the digitization of the North Carolina Studies in the Romance Languages and Literatures series.

www.ingramcontent.com/pod-product-compliance
Lightning Source LLC
Chambersburg PA
CBHW020421230426
43663CB00007BA/1261